SAY YES TO YOU

*15 Proven Steps to Set Boundaries Like a Pro
and Take Control of Your Life*

ALEKHYA KORUTI

Say Yes To You : 15 Proven Steps to Set Boundaries Like a Pro and Take Control of Your Life

ISBN: 9798871981993

To my parents, brother, husband, and daughter,

Who inspire me to dream bigger than I thought I could
.

Table of Contents

Acknowledgments

This book would not have been possible without the support and encouragement of some very important people. I would like to extend my deepest gratitude to them.

My dad, for igniting a love of books in me. That little spark fuelled my dreams of writing a book some day and here I am now. Your encouragement has always been a guiding force throughout my life.

My mom, for always, always believing in my writing, ever since I was kid. You were my first 'fan' even when my writing wasn't good and that gave me the belief that I could make writing my career. Which I did.

My brother for being the best sibling I could have asked for. Growing up with you has been one of the best things ever and your presence motivates me to excel.

My husband, for being my rock. Your boundless confidence in me, even when I doubted myself, has been my biggest reason to pursue every aspiration. Thank you for always lifting me higher than I ever thought possible.

And my darling daughter, who inspires me each day, to do better and be better. Your curiosity, innocence, and infinite joy gives me immeasurable strength and reminds me to dream big. I wake up every morning and sleep every night, hoping to make you proud.

As a new mom, this was a massive undertaking, but you all rallied so hard for me that it will forever keep me grateful. Without your support, this book would have just been another folder on my laptop.

I also want to thank my mentor and book coach, Sweta, who made me believe it was possible to write a book in the time I did. Thank you for the encouraging words you always had, for answering the silliest of questions, and for helping me realise a lifelong dream.

I must mention all my mentors who guided and trained me when I chose this path and found my calling. Their guidance and support are why I can fulfil my purpose of helping and empowering people with confidence and gratitude.

And finally, I would like to thank you for picking up this book and trusting me to help you. No amount of 'thank you' will be enough for everyone mentioned here.

This book is as much yours as it is mine.

"Speak your mind, even if your voice shakes."
-   Maggie Kuhn

ALEKHYA KORUTI

Preface

I used to believe that boundaries were bad. Real bad. I ignored them like a jilted ex-lover and avoided them like an ostrich tucking its head snuggly into the sand.

As expected, it didn't do me any good.

Only when I came across an article did I change my perspective about boundaries. It said that boundaries are like bridges. The article explained that a bridge isn't just to go back and forth; it connects two places. Every bridge comes with some restrictions like weight or entry limits. If those rules and restrictions aren't respected, even the strongest bridges can collapse under pressure.

And then, it continued to say that boundaries are akin to bridges that monitor the flow of energy and respect. The boundaries aren't there to separate but to connect, but when they aren't respected, relationships can collapse.

I thought it was an interesting read, but I never gave it much thought until a series of unfortunate incidents occurred as a result of a lack of boundaries. The article popped into my head, and the thought of important relationships collapsing scared me. That was when I even entertained the idea of setting boundaries with much hesitation and fear. That was almost a decade ago.

Now, years later, I can look back and say I'm glad I did that. It was a long road for me from that day to the present, where setting boundaries comes as second nature to me.

Over the years, I tried many tools and techniques – the ones that worked made it in the book, the ones that didn't work, well, no one needs to waste time with them.

If you are anything like that old me who believes boundaries aren't necessary, this book will change your mind. The tools and techniques shared here will definitely help you take control of your life, just like they helped me do the same.

So, chuck all your hesitation and fear of boundaries and dive in. This skill will change your life for sure.

See you on the other side of the bridge, in the place where boundaries are celebrated. Not frowned upon.

Alekhya

My Tryst With Boundaries

*"The only people who get upset about you
setting boundaries are the ones who were
benefiting from you having none."*

- Unknown

1

When was the last time you said 'No'?

If you're like the old me, I'm guessing it's probably been a while.

I bet my story will strike a chord with you. As you read, you might find yourself nodding in agreement or breaking into a knowing smile, recognizing that what I'm about to share is not just my story; it's your story too.

I genuinely wish my experiences were so unique that it would blow your mind. The reality, however, is quite the opposite. Honestly, I would have preferred it if it was different because it would mean that fewer people would have faced the challenges I'm about to discuss. Since you've picked this book, I'm pretty sure you'll resonate with my story.

So, does this sound like you?

Someone would ask you for help, and you would bend over backward to help them.
(I felt so compelled to help a hostel mate who had chickenpox when she reached out for help. I didn't even know her, but I jumped at the opportunity to help her despite being at risk of contracting the disease. I was down with chickenpox after 2 days.)

If someone asked you to join them for a gathering, you would say 'yes' even if every fibre of your being wanted to say no.

(I could have avoided so many outings but didn't. Because who was a massive people-pleaser? Me!)

If someone reached out frantically for help at an odd hour, you would drop everything for them.

(I was happy to help in most cases, but my work suffered a lot, especially when it became a habit for others to rely on me.)

We can insert dozens of similar scenarios, and the result would be the same. For both you and me.

For some reason, back then, I just couldn't say no.

It felt like a foreign word. A word made of just two alphabets seemed to have the most trouble rolling off my tongue.

Chances are you've been down this road too.

We often find ourselves in such situations because 'boundary setting' is somewhat a vague and, for many, an entirely new concept.

It's honestly a little embarrassing to admit this, but I wasn't even aware of it till my late 20s. I used to take immense pride in being the go-to person for others, available day and night. I was juggling the demands of my own life while extending my help, sometimes even to those I barely knew, without hesitation. It felt like I was burning the candle at both ends.

Don't get me wrong. I still take pride in being a 3am friend for some, and I will show up for them whenever they want, no matter what. But "some" is the key here.

After experiencing my fair share of burnout, I realized that not everyone required or deserved me to be that person. It took me quite some time to even entertain the idea of setting boundaries, but I had to do it out of necessity, not choice.

I was constantly exhausted, rarely had time to decompress, and found myself doing things that I didn't want to. Then, one day, unintentionally, I just blurted out 'no' instead of the usual 'yes'.

I feared the worst, like my friends feeling betrayed or something equally drastic, but things ended up working in my favour. Nobody took offense or felt let down. They understood, and I got my time off. It was such a strange feeling, but it was terrific.

That was the day I started going down the rabbit hole of boundary setting. The day that split my world into 'pre-boundaries era' and 'post-boundaries era.'

As I began saying yes to myself and started reaping the associated benefits, I was hooked. That's when I started setting boundaries and hoped for it to transform my life.

Only it didn't!

Because I didn't do it right. It turns out that boundary setting wasn't as simple as saying no and moving on.

My Rough Start with Boundary Setting

Before setting boundaries, I was the textbook example of a 'yes' person. Saying yes was my default mode. As I started the journey of boundary setting, I flipped the script entirely and became a 'no' machine, handing them out like I had an endless supply of this two-lettered word.

If, at first, I was letting everyone invade my space when they wished, now I was busy building walls. Neither was healthy, and I realized that boundary setting wasn't just about saying no and moving on. That it was an art, a skill which I had to learn. So, I did.

Let me tell you, it was a rocky road. I made a ton of mistakes and then some more. I got hurt at some point; I hurt a few people in the process. Some of my 'friends' couldn't handle the 'new me,' the very version of myself that made me truly happy. So, we went our separate ways. Well, no regrets!

But hey, the silver lining is that I had some awesome friends who stuck by me, no questions asked. They embraced the new and improved me with open arms and cheered me on. They saw how happy I was and pushed me to keep levelling up my boundary setting game. And guess what? These are the same friends who never took advantage of my people-pleasing phase or the 'yes' phase.

I want to give a little heads-up here – you might lose a few buddies on this boundary-setting journey. When you stop fitting into the little box they had for you and decide to break free, some of them might go the other way.

But guess what? You're better off without them. I get it; it might not feel that way at first, but trust me, I've been there with my phase of having a zillion friends, but now I've got a much smaller squad, and I've never been happier.

If you do lose some people during the journey, don't be shocked or surprised. Please take it as a sign that what you're doing is working and that you're on the right track.

In the past few years, I've realized that setting boundaries isn't an act of defiance or selfishness; it's an incredible act of self-love. The more I practiced it, the more it transformed my life for the better. As my life improved, my desire to learn about it grew, and my passion to help fellow 'yes people' struggling to draw boundaries became stronger.

This book is a product of all the lessons I learned through my personal journey and helping others. It's a result of me trying various tools and techniques, sometimes succeeding and sometimes failing. Now, I'm confident in my ability to gauge which tool will work in each scenario and what won't, and setting boundaries the right way has become second nature to me.

The tools and strategies that I covered in this book may appear small or simple at first glance, but they are incredibly powerful.

People often overlook these common, seemingly obvious strategies because they probably don't immediately realize their potential for boundary setting.

Marie Kondo says it best – part ways with things that don't bring us joy and hold onto things that do.

I applied the same principle on a much broader scale by setting boundaries. I am more at peace, have better control over my life, say yes to things that matter to me and which bring me joy, and then I truly enjoy them instead of pretending because I couldn't say no.

That is exactly what I wish to share through this book. So that you don't take as long as I took to learn to set effective boundaries or make some common mistakes.

Finally, through this book, I want to convince you that saying no and prioritizing yourself doesn't make you a bad person. That you don't have to feel guilty, awkward, or fearful. It's not only possible but also empowering, even when it feels like the last thing you want to do.

Why Trust My Decade-Long Journey?

My boundary setting journey began with Google and YouTube. I made many mistakes and did lots and lots of trial and error. I've shared what I learned over the years and what worked for me, as well as my friends, who saw great results when they applied it themselves.

Over time, I started connecting with more people who wanted to set boundaries but found themselves trapped between people-pleasing and the fear of letting others down. It was a cycle I knew all too well. I could relate to their challenges and wanted to support them.

Now, as a certified confidence and mindset coach, I get to do exactly that every day as I help people from all walks of life to set healthy boundaries.

In a perfect world, nobody would feel guilty or awkward to set boundaries and say yes to themselves. Unfortunately, the real world operates differently. I won't sugar-coat it and say that boundary setting is a piece of cake. The truth is you might not grasp it on your first attempt, and it may even feel excruciating.

But I assure you that it is absolutely possible, even for the most hesitant, sceptical, reluctant, or sensitive people. As you progress through the book, you will start or further your boundary setting journey, depending on where you're starting from, and master it.

The only difference between your journey and mine would be that yours will be much shorter with fewer mistakes.

What's In It For You?

Boundary setting is still an unfamiliar concept for many. It probably shouldn't be very surprising that some view boundary setting as harsh, unnecessary, or even unkind. This view is actually quite common in a collectivistic culture like India.

In a collectivist culture, the needs and goals of the group, such as family, community, or country, take precedence over individual desires. In countries like India, China, South Korea, Japan, Mexico, Vietnam, and Guatemala, people are considered 'good' when they prioritize the needs of others, demonstrating dependability, helpfulness, and generosity. These nations structure their social systems to support the community, family, and society rather than individual interests.

While it's wonderful to be a part of this culture, it can create pressure for those who wish to focus on themselves, even briefly. Traits like independence, assertiveness, or autonomy, which would benefit individuals but go against the 'collective' values, are frowned upon and discouraged.

It goes against the very idea that has been drilled down upon us since childhood – "_____ comes before me'. You can fill in that blank with any word, and it'll hold true – family, kids, friends, work, society, etc., etc., etc. This concept of 'everyone before you' leads to blurred personal and familial boundaries.

That's why setting boundaries feels so off for us. When we try, it feels really wrong and awful, even though we know it isn't. That's because it goes against what we've always been taught to believe.

This is also why others react the way they do when we set firm boundaries. They will not understand why you feel the need to focus on yourself or have individualistic desires. This is why they will shame, ridicule, reprimand someone trying to set boundaries, or feel extremely let down because it is the exact opposite of what we've grown up knowing and understanding.

So, do we have to completely reject the collectivist culture and adopt an individualistic approach?

No.

That would be unrealistic, unwise, impossible, and honestly, a little extreme. We just have to find the right balance, which is possible, and we can have the best of both worlds.

I'll help you do that. I am sure that you will take away at least one tool or technique that will help you set better boundaries. Once you master that technique, you can try another one. And then another. Until you master boundary setting and find yourself helping others.

I've been where you are, and I want you to reach where I am now or perhaps even further!

Roadmap for Reading This Book

In the chapters that follow, I will talk about boundary setting in personal life, relationships, family, work, and social circle. Boundary setting often come as a package deal with emotional distress where you can feel guilt, fear or even shame. We'll see how to tackle that too.

Every chapter will give you tools and techniques that will help you get one step closer to mastering boundary setting. I suggest reading the chapters in sequential order because the initial chapters help you lay the foundation, and the subsequent ones will give you clarity on how to build something strong on this foundation.

In each chapter, I'll give you some actionable steps that will make the boundary setting process more manageable without it getting overwhelming. These action steps and exercises will help you practice and apply the concepts discussed. They are designed to gradually build your skills and confidence and make boundary setting a natural part of your life.

By following these steps, you'll not only understand the theory but also experience the positive changes that boundary setting can bring to your daily life.

I want to reiterate here that all action steps discussed in the book are interconnected and reinforce each other. The tools discussed in one area can be applied to any aspect of your life, not just the one we focus on in that particular chapter.

You'll likely notice me revisiting certain points across a couple of chapters. It's all part of the plan to ensure those ideas stick with you by the time you finish the book.

By the time you turn the last page of the book, you'll become a pro at boundary setting with very little guilt - that is, if you still feel any.

One last thing that I would like to request before diving into learning all about boundary setting is to trust the process. If you do the actionable steps and spend time reflecting and refining the skills and techniques that we'll cover here, I'm sure that you will gradually master boundary-setting. It will take some time, but you'll eventually reach a place that you want to be and experience positive transformations.

Before we dive into various boundary-setting strategies, let's begin at ground zero.

This is something I wish I had known when I started setting boundaries in my own life, as it would have made the journey much smoother. Understanding these basics will help you with foundational questions such as, "Do I have boundary issues?" "Where should I set boundaries?" and "Why is setting boundaries challenging for me?"

So, let's get started.

*** *** ***

In a Nutshell

> Boundary setting journey starts with first recognizing the importance of prioritizing personal needs without guilt.
> Lack of boundaries will lead to burnout, strained relationships, stress, and dissatisfaction.
> Prioritize balanced boundaries; extremes of being overly flexible or rigid are ineffective.
> Setting boundaries may affect some relationships.
> Setting boundaries in a collectivist culture is challenging but the techniques shared in the book will help you navigate the challenges.
> Trust the process, it will give you results.

12

Exploring Boundaries

*"Boundaries aren't about keeping people
out; they're about deciding who gets in."*

— Jill Coleman

2

What's your idea of boundaries?

I wasn't aware of boundaries well into my mid-twenties. Even after I became aware, I had a very wrong idea of what they meant.

I believed I was extending kindness by always being available to help others. Little did I know, this pattern of constantly showing up for everyone else meant I was neglecting my own needs. While my intentions were good, I ended up neglecting my well-being. This selfless approach took a toll, resulting in challenges such as strained relationships and heightened stress levels.

It took me a while to understand the difference between people actually needing my help and when they are just taking advantage, who deserved the help and who didn't, and that there's a difference between people-pleasing and helping.

I knew I was missing something because there had to be a way to balance being there for others without neglecting myself.

The missing piece? Boundaries.

Let's dig deeper into this.

Understanding Boundaries

I really wish we had a penny for every time we've heard or thought, "Why set boundaries with someone you love?" Because if we did, we'd probably have a personal vault of cash ready to dive into, just like Uncle Scrooge.

Boundaries often get a bad rap. They're seen in a negative light, adorned with damaging labels. This perception stems from the widely held belief that boundaries create distance.

Well, I'm here to shift that perspective – boundaries don't keep anyone at bay. In fact, they do the exact opposite.

According to the Oxford Dictionary, a boundary is - a line that marks the edges of an area and separates it from other areas. Notice the word 'separate'. Notably, this definition doesn't imply that the separate areas need to be completely closed off from each other.

Extending that definition to the concept of boundary setting, it simply means that we opt to maintain distinct and separate areas of life. We have the choice to keep our personal life, work, friendships, and relationships segregated and define the extent to which we feel at ease intermingling them – it's all about our degree of comfort.

So, what's the first step of setting boundaries?

If you answered – saying 'no' more often, you wouldn't be entirely right. Saying 'no' is just a part of setting boundaries, but it's not the only way.

In the following chapters, we'll see how to set boundaries the right way.

The right boundaries strike a great balance between being open to others and protecting you at the same time.

Another crucial point to remember is that just setting

boundaries doesn't guarantee they're always healthy; there's a chance you might establish unhealthy ones.

So, how can you differentiate between them?

Establishing healthy boundaries can elevate your sense of well-being, putting you on cloud nine. They empower you to express your feelings and needs while showing respect for others and acknowledging their rights and boundaries.

On the flip side, unhealthy boundaries are, well, not so great. If the boundaries you establish trigger resentment, foster emotional turmoil, or strain relationships, they likely fall into the unhealthy category.

If you're new to the art of setting boundaries, you may fall into this trap. So, it's important you can differentiate between the two.

This table will help you recognize whether you are setting healthy boundaries or unhealthy boundaries.

Healthy Boundaries	Unhealthy Boundaries
Prioritises Self-Care When you can focus on self-care without feeling guilty, it's a sign of healthy boundaries. This means understanding when to say 'no' to commitments and when you need to say 'yes' for your well-being.	Manifests as Self-Neglect Setting unhealthy boundaries may manifest in behaviours that work against you. This could be ignoring your needs and desires, overextending and stretching yourself thin, or overlooking your well-being in favour of others.

You Have Clear Values and Priorities When you are absolutely sure of your values and priorities, you will end up setting healthy boundaries. These help you understand what's important and help align your decisions with what truly matters to you.	**You Struggle with a Lack of Self-Identity** If you feel like you lost yourself in relationships, when you don't remember the last time you asserted your individuality, and know that you always conform to the expectations and needs of others, then there are very high chances that you have unhealthy boundaries.
You Feel at Peace Setting healthy boundaries is rooted in self-respect, honouring your emotional and mental limitations, recognizing your self-worth, and respecting your personal boundaries. When you make decisions keeping all these at the core, you will almost always feel at peace. You will have higher emotional stability, increased self-confidence, and stronger relationships.	**You Are Constantly Anxious or Stressed** Ever felt like you didn't do enough even if you did the absolute best you could? It could be the inner voice talking or someone else expressing disappointment that you could have done better. If you chase perfectionism and indulge in excessive self-criticism, it's probably because you set unhealthy boundaries. All of this will leave you feeling stressed and anxious most of the time. Your emotional stability will be low, and you will start being resentful.

As I was writing this, two stories came to mind that are perfect examples of people setting unhealthy relationships.

When I first met Radhika, she was already deep into setting unhealthy boundaries without realising it. She thought she was setting the right boundaries but didn't understand why she felt so isolated and lonely.

She was making one mistake most people make when it comes to setting boundaries.

Radhika had a humongous friend circle. In fact, she had multiple friend circles and was always hanging out with one group or the other. She believed that they all were very close and went to the extent of calling these friends her safety net. She thought that these people would always be around to catch her when she stumbled in life. She gave them her all. She kept giving and giving because "that's what friends did, right?"

Until she realised that no one shared this belief with her. She saw that everyone thought of her as just a friend, not really a close friend. She noticed that she couldn't lean on anyone during some hard times and watched her friends prioritise partying more than helping her.

What was worse was that they ridiculed her when she wanted to discuss an issue that was bothering her. Instead of supporting and hearing her out, they insisted she was bringing their entire group's mood down by talking about her sob story.

She thought they were right and stopped sharing. She continued to meet them, still partied or shopped or brunched with them, but now it was starting to feel more like a chore than fun. She wasn't just hesitant to share her problems but also the good stuff because no one really seemed excited to hear her out.

It started with her saying no to a few social commitments here and there, and she started maintaining some distance. She saw that it served her well, so she pressed her feet on the accelerator and took it to the other extreme. She completely cut everyone off and never told them how their actions and behaviour bothered her.

Here's the mistake she made – she started building walls in the name of setting boundaries.

Building the metaphorical wall is a protective mechanism or a coping strategy. It is not boundary setting. When Radhika started building walls, it affected her loved ones too.. From being the 'yes friend', she parked herself on the other end of the spectrum where she only said 'no' even to her loved ones. No wonder she felt isolated!

Boundaries are only supposed to separate and not isolate. They help you form healthy and respectful relationships, but they never isolate.

You know what does isolate? Walls. Sure, you can feel secure behind a wall because it's great at keeping the hurt and disappointment out. But walls also keep love, joy, and healthy social relationships away.

When I first met Radhika, she was an anxious person who rarely smiled anymore. She spoke with a deep sadness and believed she would never have good friends.

Then, she learned the difference between boundaries and walls. She figured out that what she was doing, even though it seemed good for her, wasn't the right way. She might not be completely ready to break down all those walls, but she has started making a few changes and is seeing real changes. And the best part? She's smiling again because she doesn't feel isolated anymore!

Another person that comes to mind when I think of unhealthy boundaries is Priyanka. If I thought I was a 'yes person', she was miles ahead in another league. She stretched herself so thin just because she hated saying no. In fact, saying 'no' made her physically sick. She would start to shiver, stammer, or even throw up at the thought of saying no.

That definitely is an extreme case, but there are people like that. She was a dear friend, and I had no clue how to help her because I wasn't aware of boundary setting myself at the time. So, just like any good friend, I enabled her 'yes syndrome' and just helped her through the physical discomfort the best way I could.

Today, she's doing much better. She actually needed a therapist's help to get over this because it was affecting her life so much. There were deeper issues that exacerbated her discomfort with boundary setting. She's still a work in progress, but I'm glad to say that she can say 'no', at least without wanting to throw up!

Radhika, Priyanka, and I now know why we had trouble setting boundaries. One big issue was that we didn't think we needed boundaries in the first place.

If you're not sure about your own boundaries, now is a good time to take a quick test. It'll show you if you need boundaries or not.

Be honest!

1. Ever said "yes" too much just to please others and ended up feeling like a one-person show trying to meet everyone's needs?

2. Ever reluctantly agreed to things you didn't want to do, like dancing even if you absolutely hate dancing or agreeing to a lunch commitment when staying home seemed cosier, all because saying 'no' felt tougher?

3. You're invited to a spontaneous movie night, but you'd rather snuggle in PJs with a good book. Do you find it easier to reluctantly say 'yes' to the cinema than to say 'no'?

4. Did someone's drama invade your emotional space, disturbing your peace because you felt obligated to be supportive?

5. Ever had the urge to express your needs but ended up with a jumble of emojis and incomplete sentences?

6. Felt anger or frustration because you placed others' needs above your own and ended up with resentment?

7. Do you feel stuck in a cycle of sacrifice because that's what society expects from a good friend/partner/employee/parent/family member?

8. Are you a devoted people-pleaser, making everyone's dreams come true except your own? (Bonus points if you've pulled last-minute miracles for others at the cost of your well-being).

9. Have you ever grappled with the internal tug-of-war between wanting to exit a toxic relationship, be it romantic, one-way friendships, or family ties, and preserving your own well-being and peace of mind but choosing toxicity because it's easier than saying yes to yourself?

10. Have you ever struggled to communicate your boundaries, leaving your needs unspoken and your feelings bottled up, all to avoid conflict or displeasing others?

If you said yes to any one of these, then you, my friend, need to work on your boundary settings. Don't feel overwhelmed about not knowing how or where to start.

Understanding that you need boundary setting is the very first step, and you did that!

Everything from here on will help you with the '*how*'. Like I already said, just trust the process, and by the end of this book, you will be comfortable with boundary setting.

Now, let's look at another huge reason why people aren't very successful at boundary setting.

Boundary Myths

A second reason why most of us fail at boundary setting is because we believe in the many myths that surround 'boundaries.'

In fact, these myths were a significant contributing factor to why Priyanka would always have such a visceral reaction to even the thought of setting boundaries. These misconceptions triggered a flood of negative emotions in her, especially guilt.

If just the thought of setting boundaries is already causing clammy hands and making you feel uneasy, consider whether you, like Priyanka, might be buying into one of the common myths associated with boundaries.

So, why don't we bust some of them?

- Boundaries are selfish.
  No, they aren't. Boundaries are essential for self-care and maintaining healthy relationships.

- Boundaries are supposed to be fixed, static, and rigid.
  False, boundaries are flexible and permeable to allow for healthy interactions. They evolve over time and never stay static.

- Boundaries are a sign of weakness.
  It couldn't be further away from the truth. Boundaries are a sign of self-awareness and strength.

- Boundaries can ruin relationships.
  Well, boundaries often strengthen relationships and build respectful connections. If they ruin any relationship, you probably are better without it.

- Boundaries must be the same for everyone.
  False again. Boundaries should be tailored to different scenarios, people, and circumstances. You cannot have the same boundaries for every situation and relationship.

Another common assumption people make is that boundaries should be obvious to others. You will only hurt yourself if you assume that others should automatically know what your boundaries are just because you share a close relationship. You need to communicate your boundaries clearly and not rely on someone just knowing it.

And lastly, don't fall into the trap of believing that boundaries are unnecessary in close relationships. In fact, you definitely need boundaries in close relationships because they are crucial for maintaining mutual respect and strengthening the bond.

Signs of Poor Boundaries

Another step you need to take when you start setting boundaries is identifying if you have poor boundaries to begin with. This will help you get a clear understanding of the path ahead and the effort you need to put in.

I stumbled upon an insightful video by Dr. Ramani Durvasula, a renowned clinical psychologist, who identified these 9 behaviours as signs of poor boundaries. I was genuinely surprised to learn this, as I had never associated these behaviours with poor boundaries.

Of course, displaying these behaviours doesn't mean that it's solely a result of poor boundaries, but it's crucial to understand that it could be.

1. Inability to make decisions
2. People pleasing
3. Excessive fatigue
4. Endless guilt about small things
5. Lost sense of self
6. Oversharing
7. Resentment towards partners boundaries
8. Passive aggressive
9. Fear of rejection or abandonment

Do you have any of these signs or behaviours? If yes, then self-analyse if it is a result of poor boundary setting or if some other aspect is in play.

Radhika and Priyanka definitely displayed a few of these behaviours and believed the common myths. If they were aware of the same, they could have avoided a lot of heartache and pain.

Another thing they wish they were aware of was that boundaries aren't supposed to be all or nothing. When you set boundaries, it's important to strike the right balance that allows you to feel happy without making others feel isolated or vice versa. It doesn't have to be only about you or all about others.

Success with boundary setting won't happen overnight. It's a muscle you need to work on; the more you work to build it, the better you get at it. It's similar to starting a fitness routine.

At first, you might not feel like doing it, or you could be excited because it's new and promises better health. Then, you start and, at some point, feel like quitting because it's not easy. But if you stick with it, you'll notice a difference and eventually reach your goals. What seemed hard initially becomes easy because you've built the strength to handle it.

The same principle applies to setting boundaries. Make sure to stick with it even after you've mastered it. If you ditch your plan once you reach your goals and opt to be the equivalent of a couch potato, you'll have to start all over again.

Setting boundaries will only bring you benefits, with the only condition being that you establish healthy boundaries, not unhealthy ones.

If you still need a bit more convincing about why setting boundaries is crucial, the following analogy will solidify your belief.

The Garden Fence Analogy

The Garden Fence analogy is one of the best I've come across to explain boundaries. The genius of this analogy, which was given by Dr. Sarah Davies, a renowned psychologist, lies in its simplicity.

Imagine this.

You have built your dream house in your dream location. Every detail in your property is just like you wanted. You have a huge garden in front of your house, and to protect this garden and house, you build a small fence around it.

This fence is approachable and non-threatening. It is low enough for others to see you and not be closed off but high enough to offer you safety and security. The job of the fence is to mark your property and separate it from others' or public land.

Those who see the fence will innately understand that they cannot just jump over and trespass into your beautiful garden. Nothing about the fence will offend them because it is a part of the property. They will automatically honour it.

Now, imagine there was no fence. People would come in and out of your garden with no regard for the property. They could argue that they didn't realise it was your garden because nothing separated it from the public street. Their argument would be right. It's upon you to build the fence for others' understanding.

Now, consider building a towering wall instead of a fence around your house. It sends a clear message: "Please stay out." With no visibility, you remain secluded, unaware if someone is reaching out or wants to come inside. This is just as harmful as having no fence at all. While you enjoy your beautiful house in solitude, you miss out on sharing the joy of building your dream home with others.

This is exactly what boundaries are. Just like the fence, the right kind of boundaries tells others, firmly and clearly, what is acceptable and what isn't without being rigid. The first time someone entered your garden without your permission, you wouldn't fly off the handle but rather ask them to leave politely. But if it repeats all the time, then it's a different story.

Apply the same for boundaries. Clear boundaries won't offend anyone, unclear or inconsistent boundaries will only confuse others and frustrate you, and building rigid boundaries or walls will keep everyone away. Boundaries are simply a way to honour your priorities and needs without shutting others out.

When it comes to setting boundaries, the key is to stick to them. Just like you'd make sure your garden fence stays in good shape, you've got to consistently work on keeping your boundaries intact. You can't have them one day, change them the next, or take them away completely and then wonder why things aren't going as expected.

If you find it hard to stick to your boundaries, you might end up being easily influenced. It's easy to play the blame game, but it's crucial to take accountability for your boundaries and ensure you maintain them rather than pointing fingers at others.

You have to identify which areas of your life need boundaries and assess if the existing boundaries are healthy or unhealthy. It won't be a surprise if you're a pro at setting boundaries in one area, but a total amateur in another.

So, why don't we change that. Let's jump in and get to work!

ACTIVITY 1: The Garden Fence Exercise

To begin any journey, you need to know where you stand and where you need to go. This exercise will help you understand that. You'll identify which boundaries you lack and need to work on.

You have to connect the garden fence analogy to your life.

Do a small relaxation exercise before you start. It could be meditation, dancing, or listening to a favourite song. Whatever helps you get in a positive and relaxed state of mind, please do it.

Now, imagine yourself in your safe space with a fence around. Think of a personal encounter or a recent situation in which you felt that this 'fence' was crossed without permission. This might have involved a conversation, an action, or someone's behaviour. It could have occurred with a friend, a family member, a co-worker, or even a stranger. Now, vividly replay that scenario in your mind as if it were unfolding in real-time.

If several incidents pop into your mind, choose one that bothered you the most. Write about how you felt when it happened. Pay attention to the thoughts and emotions you experience. Specifically, pinpoint what about that incident made you feel uncomfortable.

If thoughts or emotions aren't immediately apparent, focus on any sensations in your body. Don't overlook the signals your body provides; they're one of the most reliable ways to understand if your boundaries have been crossed.

This might require going deep and allowing yourself to fully experience whatever comes up. Physical sensations are an excellent way to identify boundary violations. They are a result of the subconscious but are almost always accurate.

It often happens that in the heat of the moment, you might not notice if a boundary was crossed. It's only when you take a step back to reflect or introspect that you recognize different instances where your boundaries were completely disregarded. That's why this can be such a powerful exercise.

Getting the hang of it may take a little while, but try it out with different scenarios to understand which boundaries you need to set for yourself or work on more.

Take your time with this step—don't rush it. Journal in detail, list it out on your phone, or make quick notes on your laptop; choose whatever works for you, but don't skip this step.

It's possible to feel a bit overwhelmed after this exercise if you see that you may need to set many boundaries in different areas. Let's just pause there for a bit.

The pro tip shared in the next segment will help you navigate through this overwhelm.

Expand the Comfort Zone Gradually

You don't have to start big or do it all at once. You cannot cover the entire ground on day one. Take just one step.

Identify and choose a small boundary that feels manageable for you to set. If starting with a friend feels challenging, consider practicing with someone less familiar, like declining an invitation from an acquaintance such as a colleague or distant relative, making it a relatively easier step.

Once you decide what boundary to establish, give yourself a timeframe to do it and stick to it. Otherwise, you will keep procrastinating, essentially bringing you back to square one.

Upon the completion of the step, reflect on your experience. How did it make you feel to expand your comfort zone? Identify if it helped you learn something about yourself, boundary setting, or the process.

Feeling discomfort is natural, especially based on your comfort level with setting boundaries. You might not enjoy the emotions arising from asserting a boundary, and self-judgment may creep in. Approach this exercise with utmost self-compassion, as if you were an outsider observing someone else. Release the urge to criticize and embrace the process with understanding and kindness toward yourself.

Look at it this way - Boundary setting is all about energy management. It empowers you to preserve your energy battery. Set boundaries wisely and surround yourself with individuals who contribute to keeping your battery charged.

I would recommend you to identify some 'boundary buddies' at this stage. These are family members or friends, who have your best interest at heart and can support you in your boundary setting journey. They can help you execute the exercises and action steps shared in the chapters. This works well if you aren't comfortable doing the exercises alone and also adds in a layer of accountability.

One last thing to remember before we dive in - Boundaries need to come with consequences; otherwise, they're just wishful thinking. If someone doesn't respect your boundaries, it's crucial to establish consequences that align with the boundary they've crossed.

Now that you know how boundaries work, let's dive into a chapter that's all about 'YOU'. Setting boundaries begins in your personal life and then ripples into other areas.

Feeling nervous? I've got your back.

Excited? I'm right here cheering you on!

*** *** ***

In a Nutshell

> Boundaries are only supposed to separate and not isolate.
> Healthy boundaries empower you and help foster positive relationships, and unhealthy boundaries lead to resentment and emotional turmoil.
> Identifying signs of poor boundaries gives a starting point to self-analyse and recognize areas for improvement.
> The right boundaries strike a balance between being open to others and protecting you at the same time.
> Don't assume people will know what your boundaries are.
> Start small, be consistent.
> Build the muscle of boundary setting through consistent practice

Prioritizing Personal Boundaries

"Setting boundaries is a way of caring for myself. It doesn't make me mean, selfish, or uncaring because I don't do things your way. I care about me too."

— Christine Morgan

3

This chapter is all about setting personal boundaries. It is all about you and the kind of boundaries you want in your personal life.

In the last two chapters, we laid the groundwork by understanding what exactly boundaries are, which boundaries you probably would like to set or work on, or which boundaries others are violating. But we've just scratched the surface.

If you are still unsure, by the end of this chapter, you will have a pretty clear idea. Let's start by exploring everything you need to know about personal boundaries, understanding what categories different boundaries fall under, and how you can effectively communicate those boundaries to others.

To kick off this chapter on personal boundaries, I'd like to share a reel example that I found to be just as impactful as the real examples I have in my kitty.

I'd like to remind you of Rani, the protagonist of the movie 'Queen'. In Kangana Ranaut's character, we witnessed a powerful transformation as she sets personal boundaries throughout the film.

After her wedding got called off, she bravely embarked on a solo European honeymoon because it was something she desired. Rani stayed true to herself, identified her wants and needs, emerging much stronger.

Recognizing her happiness, she drew a boundary, choosing not to reconcile with her ex-fiancé, even when he expressed a desire to reunite, despite societal expectations suggesting otherwise. While a reconciliation might have garnered societal approval, Rani prioritized her own happiness, making a bold and empowering decision that resonates with the theme of setting personal boundaries.

Just as you probably cheered on Rani in her journey, it's time to be your own cheerleader now as you step into the domain of personal boundaries.

Categories of Boundaries

Have you ever taken a wild guess at how many boundary categories exist? I confess, I horribly under-guessed, and it turns out I'm not alone. Most folks I've helped or worked with usually thought there were just two or three.

But guess what? There are actually six! Surprising, right? Let's take a look.

1. Physical Boundaries

These are boundaries that you set around your personal space, your body, and physical needs like food and rest.

Questions to help you explore physical boundaries

- How comfortable am I when others give me a hug or am I only comfortable with handshakes?
- Who am I comfortable hugging, and with whom do I want to keep a physical distance?
- Am I comfortable with others entering my personal space (house room, work areas, any other space), or is that space just for me/a few select people?
- Are there specific foods, drinks, or habits that I'm not comfortable indulging in? This might include situations involving smoking, varied food preferences, or alcohol

consumption.

- How much do I prioritise my need to rest, and how will I do that?

Recognising physical boundary violations

- When others enter a personal space, like a home office or bedroom, without your permission.
- Someone hugs or touches you without your consent and makes you uncomfortable despite you conveying it.
- When someone insists or forces you to eat something you don't want, disregarding your preferences.
- People not respecting your non-verbal cues, like stepping back or avoiding physical contact.
- Someone dismissing your need to take a break and coercively pushing you into activities you'd rather avoid.

My friends and I are huge huggers! We love giving hugs to everyone who's comfortable with them. But we are also aware of those who don't like hugs, so we give high-fives or handshakes with equal enthusiasm.

If you are anything like us, you would want to share the joy of hugs with everyone, but let's not impose it on others just because we love them and feel they are harmless. It's always better to ask someone what they are comfortable with.

2. Emotional Boundaries

These are boundaries you establish regarding what you're comfortable sharing emotionally with others. You can't be vulnerable with everyone, and emotional boundaries centre on respecting both your emotions and those of others. It's essential to understand how much emotional energy you're willing to invest and be mindful of what, when, and with whom to share.

Equally important is the awareness of when to consciously refrain from emotional sharing, particularly with those who don't respect your established boundaries.

Questions to help you explore emotional boundaries

- Who do I feel comfortable reaching out to when I have something personal to share? Who do I prefer not to reach out to at all?
- What am I comfortable sharing with friends, family, and others?
- Is someone holding space for me when I'm sharing something personal, or are they being dismissive about my feelings? How would I like to handle the latter?
- How do I manage my own emotions so that even when I'm vulnerable and sharing my issues with others, I don't end up putting the entire load on them?
- How will I react when someone overwhelms me with their emotional dump or when I'm in no capacity to process their issues?

Recognising emotional boundary violations

- When someone dismisses or criticises your feelings and emotions.
- When someone poses a question that makes you uncomfortable or asks something inappropriate, considering the level of comfort in the relationship.
- Emotional dumping of info or news on you without your permission or checking if you are up for it.
- Someone telling you how you should feel or asking you to justify why you feel a certain way.
- Sharing inappropriate emotional information with your family members without your knowledge, especially with children who are incapable of differentiating between truth and gossip.

If you're reading this book, chances are you find yourself in this category. Perhaps you feel like a punching bag where everyone unloads their drama or emotions on you, and it seems like no one is really listening, leaving you unsure of how to politely say no.

But don't worry; we're going to change that in the chapters ahead.

3. Time Boundaries

These are boundaries you set to protect, utilise or prioritise your time.

If you are the yes person who gives all their time to someone else, leaving yourself very little to no time for yourself, you need to work on your time boundaries.

Questions to help you explore time boundaries

- When I have free time, what do I prioritise in that?
- How much time do I keep aside for myself to focus on my well-being, rest, or hobbies, interests, and passions?
- If someone asks me to extend myself time-wise, how often do I give in?
- What happens when I'm repeatedly asked to work overtime or dumped with last-minute deadlines with an expectation to finish anyhow, even if it means sacrificing family or personal time and health?

Recognising time boundary violations

- People make unrealistic demands on your time, placing excessive expectations on what you can accomplish.
- When someone habitually shows up late or fails to respect your time commitments.
- When others consistently ignore or neglect agreed-upon timelines, which in turn impacts your ability to manage time effectively.
- Continuously calling you even after being informed about your unavailability at a specific time, such as after work hours.
- Consistently assigning additional work to you at the last minute.

When I was living in Pune, I knew this person who would say yes to every single work and personal commitment. She was always rushing from some work event or last-minute work to a party that her friends or acquaintances invited her to because she felt it was rude to say no.

She was constantly on the move, barely getting time to eat or rest. On some occasions, she tried leaving early, and she was 'jokingly' called names for not staying until the end.

Though she stuck to her commitments, even when it wasn't always easy for her, she rarely felt appreciated. Over time, she got stretched thin, which started affecting her health. She had to take a long, hard look at what drained her energy and what she needed to do for her own well-being instead of spending her free time in a cab on a heavily trafficked road listening to unfortunate music choices of the cab driver.

That's when she began cutting back on some commitments, feeling happier and more in control of her life.

4. Sexual Boundaries

Setting healthy sexual boundaries involves actively establishing guidelines for sexual well-being and fostering clear communication to express personal limits.

Healthy sexual boundaries are a mix of consent, respect, agreement, and privacy, along with understanding each other's preferences and limitations. It may include seeking approval, declining activities you aren't comfortable with, and safeguarding the privacy of the other person if that's their preference.

Questions to help you explore sexual boundaries

- How do I communicate consent verbally and non-verbally?
- What are my limits when it comes to sexual safety?
- How do I feel about intimacy with someone, and how can I communicate if I don't feel comfortable at any point?
- What actions or situations make me feel most comfortable or uncomfortable in an intimate setting?

- How do I navigate and communicate boundaries when it comes to exploring new aspects of intimacy with a partner?

Recognising sexual boundary violations

- Getting unwanted sexual comments.
- Someone getting angry when you don't give consent.
- Guilting you into intimacy or pressuring you to be intimate.
- Unwanted touch or assault.
- Lying about the health history, especially if it can harm the other person.

Fortunately, I personally don't know anyone who has faced sexual boundary violations from someone they know. However, the unfortunate reality is that women experience it every day, regardless of their geographical location. Acts like catcalling are a violation of sexual boundaries, not to mention other, more severe offenses.

5. Intellectual Boundaries

These boundaries are centred on your ideas, thoughts, and curiosity. They guide you in deciding how to react when someone disrespects your thoughts and ideas, how you communicate with others, and how you show respect for their ideas. They can be violated when your ideas, thoughts, and curiosity are dismissed, ridiculed, or belittled.

Having intellectual boundaries also means that you understand when it is a good time to talk about something and when to park it for some other time.

Questions to help you explore intellectual boundaries

- What'll I do when someone dismisses my ideas and thoughts?
- What will I do if a friendly debate crosses a line? Will I walk away and remove myself from the situation or continue?

- How will I communicate to someone that my ideas and thoughts aren't being respected?
- How will I convey to others that I want to remove myself from a conversation without escalating tensions?

Recognising intellectual boundary violations

- Dismissing or belittling your ideas or thoughts.
- Laughing at or mocking your curiosity.
- Disregarding your need for a pause in discussing certain topics.
- Disrespecting your opinions or viewpoints.
- Insisting on discussing a topic even when you've expressed discomfort.
- Undermining your intellectual capabilities or questioning your knowledge.

You're not obligated to embrace others' thoughts and opinions if they don't align with your values. The point is not to belittle or mock them for those thoughts. However, when someone introduces inherently harmful or sensitive topics like racism, xenophobia, or sexism, clearly express that you prefer not to delve into such discussions.

Handling conversations about sensitive personal matters and diverse opinions is a key aspect of healthy communication. But if someone is deliberately spreading hate or negativity for no reason, it's important to set boundaries. You can choose to end the conversation and distance yourself from the situation.

Setting intellectual boundaries might feel weird, but the reality is that some individuals might feel threatened by your thoughts or opinions, resorting to cheap, belittling tactics. I experienced this first-hand when someone ridiculed me for having a broader vocabulary than them. At that moment, my response was a simple 'What's wrong with that?' which sort of silenced them. However, the incident lingered in my mind because I never expected someone to have an issue with something like that and mock me in a hurtful manner.

You must have seen this, right? People teasing or making fun of someone just because their opinions are different or because they know more about a certain topic. It's sad to see this happen, especially when differences in ideas should lead to positive discussions rather than belittling or mocking each other.

6. Material Boundaries

These are boundaries pertaining to your material possessions like clothes, home, jewellery, money, etc. You should establish clear boundaries about what you're comfortable sharing and how you expect others to treat your belongings when they have them.

Questions to help you explore material boundaries

- What am I willing to share?
- With whom am I comfortable sharing all my things or certain things?
- What are the things that are absolutely off-limits?
- Is something too precious or expensive for me to share, and how can I say no when someone asks to borrow it?

Recognising material boundary violations

- When the person who borrows your possessions destroys or steals them.
- When someone borrows something without your permission.
- When someone borrows an item and doesn't return it within an agreed-upon timeframe.
- When your personal items are used to control or manipulate you, such as withholding or hiding your personal belongings to gain leverage.

I've lived with over a two dozen roommates over the course of a decade, and each one of us had different material boundaries with each other. While some of us were perfectly comfortable raiding into each other's wardrobes with prior intimation, others didn't like anyone taking their possessions, even in their presence. And we were completely okay with that. As long as we communicated material boundaries with each other, everything was smooth sailing.

Another example that comes to mind is my bookworm circle. We are all extremely possessive of our books. So much so that we have lent our cars, jewellery, or other expensive things to our friends without a second thought but always said no when we had to lend books.

We only lend it to a select few who we know would keep the books in the exact condition we would give them. They respect the books the same way and don't return them with coffee mug stains and food crumbs.

While some laughed at us or found this hard boundary to be a little crazy, they did not get offended when we refused to lend it to them. They respected it.

*** *** ***

I'll let you in on a secret.

People will respect our boundaries if we clearly communicate them! We always feel that others will get offended or feel bad when we set boundaries. But in reality, in most cases, people are more than happy to honour the boundaries without minding or challenging them.

Communication is key to effective boundary setting. You cannot expect people to just know or be mind-readers, even if it's someone extremely close to you or has known you for a long time.

Unless the person is really inconsiderate of everyone, or believes it's ridiculous to ask, apologise or take permission from family or friends, most will honour the boundaries.

Boundaries aren't a 'one-size-fits-all' concept. The flexibility or rigidity of your boundaries depends on the depth of your relationships. Holding the same boundary for everyone is impractical and unfair. Your relationships evolve, and so should your boundaries. Each person in your life may require different boundaries. It's okay to be comfortable with certain things with certain people without extending those boundaries to everyone.

Even if you're comfortable with some people and have extremely flexible boundaries for them, it's still a good idea to discuss each other's boundaries. A minor miscommunication can ruin things, and you wouldn't want that with someone so close. Even in the strongest friendships, there will be certain aspects around which you'll have boundaries.

I'll repeat once again - always communicate!

You now understand the different layers of boundary setting. But you cannot set boundaries without a reason. Yes, you need to know your '*why*' when it comes to setting boundaries. When you set boundaries with a clear reason, it's easy to maintain and hold boundaries.

When you don't know why you are setting boundaries, you will be lenient or loose with them. Then, those boundaries won't hold, and you'll go back to where you started.

This is where self-awareness comes in.

The Importance of Self-Awareness

You probably didn't expect the concept of self-awareness to pop up in the middle of boundaries conversation. But if you think about it, self-awareness is kind of a prerequisite to boundary setting.

Self-awareness will help you understand why you wish to have certain boundaries with someone, recognise when they are crossed, what you'll do when they are crossed, and acknowledge the associated feelings. Self-awareness will also help you understand if your boundaries are too rigid or too flexible and help you identify areas for improvement.

Look at the list from Activity 1, where you outlined the various boundaries you'd like to set. Now, categorize them into the six categories we discussed.

Drawing inspiration from the fence analogy, envision your garden where some areas are thriving well (representing boundaries you've effectively set and maintained) while others may need more attention (signifying boundaries that require further development or establishment). There's no absolute right or wrong; the goal is to recognize where your focus is needed.

Evaluate your existing boundaries and note the ones that are strong and those that require improvement. Reflect on experiences, incidents, and interactions that made you feel uncomfortable or violated, even to a small extent. Identify the frequency of such occurrences, your responses, and the impact they have on your well-being.

You might observe that there are some situations where upholding your boundaries is always challenging, so it keeps repeating. These repetitive scenarios are what we refer to as 'patterns.' Identifying these patterns is the initial step toward addressing them effectively.

To quote Tony Robbins, "The greatest benefit to recognizing patterns is that it gives you a pathway to power and a ladder out of chaos."

In essence, understanding patterns gives you an insight into why a repeated behaviour is occurring and how to proactively change that before it impacts your well-being.

Identifying Values and Priorities

Do you now have an idea of which boundaries you need to enforce, set, or work upon based on the activities we've done?

If you don't and are still finding the whole process overwhelming, doing what Rajat did will help you.

When first introduced to the concept of setting boundaries, he found himself overwhelmed and uncertain about where to begin. Despite acknowledging the necessity of establishing boundaries for his well-being, he procrastinated for days without taking any action. It was during this period that he discovered one of the most effective hacks for boundary setting – turning to values and priorities.

Your values and priorities act as your north star, as a compass to guide you through life. Even if you don't have any clue about boundaries, you will definitely have a list of values and priorities that are clear in your head. Don't hesitate to lean on them as they can influence the kind of boundaries that you need to set and determine your choices.

Once Rajat figured out that he could align his boundaries with his priorities and values, setting them became a breeze. Before that, he was stuck and struggled for days.

How Values and Priorities Guide Boundary Setting

Values are deeply held beliefs and principles that influence our attitudes and actions. They serve as guiding standards by which we judge what is right or wrong, and they shape our choices and behaviours. These could be honesty, kindness, integrity, respect, responsibility, compassion, or any other principles that you hold dear to your heart.

Priorities highlight the areas in our lives that take precedence over others. For some, it's their career. For others, it's their relationships, personal growth, health, or even their community involvement.

ACTIVITY 2 - Assess Your Values and Priorities

This activity is all about getting clarity about your values and priorities, which in turn help you set boundaries that align with your values. Even if you know which boundaries you want to set, it's a good idea to do this activity as it may give you some new insight.

Here's what you need to do:

- Find a quiet spot where you can think without distractions.
- Get a notebook, or use your phone or computer to write down your thoughts.
- Now, think about the things that matter to you the most in life. Note down the words or phrases that describe them. Write them in order of importance they are to you.
- Reflect and explain why each of these is important to you.
- Look at your list and make sure it really represents what matters to you. Rework if required.
- Keep in mind that this list will act as your compass for setting boundaries and help you make decisions that align with what's most important to you.

This step will surely give you a very clear idea of which boundaries you need to set and why. There is a chance that you may wonder if you're setting the right boundaries or not. If that question is circling your mind, here's a clear way to figure that out.

If your boundaries align with your values and priorities, you will feel a sense of calm.

If they don't, you will feel conflicted, uneasy, or drained out.

As I mentioned in the first chapter, tune into what your body is telling you. It will give you very clear signs.

Personal Boundaries and Self-Esteem

Have you ever thought about how personal boundaries and self-esteem go hand in hand?

When you establish healthy boundaries, you're telling the world that your needs matter, boosting your self-esteem in the process.

With high self-esteem, you'll naturally identify more boundaries you want to set and confidently uphold them.

It's like this positive loop where reinforcing boundaries enhances self-esteem, and the more confident you become, the better you get at navigating relationships and situations.

Conversely, a lack of boundaries can lead to a drop in self-esteem, making it easy for others to take advantage of your time and energy, chipping away at your self-worth.

Understanding this connection reminds us to nurture boundaries and self-esteem for our overall mental and emotional well-being.

Now, if increased self-worth is the outcome of boundary setting, then self-care is the catalyst.

Self-Care as a Foundation

"Self-care is not a luxury; it's a necessity. And setting boundaries is an essential part of self-care." - Jodi Picoult

I thought I was a pro in self-care. I loved getting massages, warm showers, good books, aromatherapy, and binge-watching a comedy after a long, hard day. Well, that was my idea of self-care.

Turns out, I was wrong.

While mindlessly scrolling on Instagram, I came across a reel that burst this notion in precisely 10 seconds. It really made me rethink a lot of what I thought self-care was.

It said that everything I equated with self-care was actually self-indulgence!

Before I tell you the difference between the two, I think I should address a question that probably popped up in your head — now, why did self-care come right in the middle of learning about boundary setting?

Well, boundary setting is a form of self-care!

In fact, self-care is the cornerstone upon which strong boundaries are built. It's like the foundation upon which your entire dream life can be built.

Without it, everything can crumble. It may sound dramatic, but it is true. Once you visualised your fence and dream house, you need to start building the foundation to build your dream house.

This is where self-care comes in. Let's see how different it is from self-indulgence.

	Self-Indulgence	Self-Care
Definition	Excessive focus on personal desires and pleasures. It's often a short-term gratification.	Deliberate actions to maintain and improve physical, mental, and emotional well-being.
Motivation	Driven by immediate pleasure and enjoyment without considering the negative consequences.	Motivated by long-term well-being and self-preservation.
Frequency	May occur frequently, leading to overindulgence.	Regular and consistent, integrated into one's routine.
Consequences	Can lead to negative outcomes, such as guilt, regret, or negative health consequences.	Results in overall positive effects on physical and mental health, enhanced relationships, and stress reduction.

Balance	Often lacks balance and can border on impulsivity.	Focused on maintaining balance and moderation in various aspects of life.
Long-Term Impact	Typically, it leads to emotional and physical burnout, strained relationships, and mental stress.	Promotes emotional resilience, improved mental health, and a sense of self-worth.
Examples	Overeating, excessive spending, indulging in addictive behaviours or neglecting responsibilities.	Exercise, meditation, spending time with loved ones, maintaining a balanced diet, and getting quality sleep.

Self-care is all about engaging in activities that boost or benefit our emotional, mental, and physical well-being in the long run. It might be tough initially, but it is always beneficial in the long run. Self-care is about making conscious choices with a lot of thought and intention and is always focused on your well-being.

Self-indulgence is engaging in behaviours that have instant gratification but may not necessarily have positive outcomes in the long run. In fact, it may even have some negative impact or outcomes in the long run.

For instance, watching Netflix well into the night is an act of self-indulgence because it's fun, and you can justify that you had a rough, long, busy day, so you deserve it (my favourite way to self-indulge). Short-term benefit. But the next day, you will struggle to get through the day at work (I can vouch for this because I always regret this decision).

Self-care, on the other hand, is about sleeping in early so that your body and mind recover and are well prepared to take on another day positively.

Self-care is a very proactive choice. You have to stay on top of it. Self-indulgence is passive; you don't have to think about it and just go with the flow just because it feels good.

Don't get me wrong. Self-indulgence is absolutely necessary!

After all, we all deserve to have a guilt-free binge-watching session, spas and massages, and whatnot. The point is, first, focus on self-care, and you can practice as much self-indulgence as you want after that. If you just focus on the latter and completely disregard the former, you will not have a solid foundation for sustaining your well-being.

The key lies in recognizing that self-care involves more than just indulging in pleasures; it encompasses activities and practices that genuinely nourish your physical, mental, and emotional health.

Whether it's getting enough sleep, eating nourishing meals, engaging in activities that bring you joy, or setting and maintaining healthy boundaries, these are the building blocks of a robust self-care routine. Once you prioritize self-care, you'll find that the moments of self-indulgence become even more meaningful and contribute positively to your overall well-being.

Setting boundaries may not always feel pleasant in the beginning, and that's okay. It might be uncomfortable, and you may not enjoy it at first. But focus on the long-term benefits that far outweigh the initial discomfort.

On the flip side, if you avoid setting boundaries because you want to avoid short-term awkwardness and prioritize immediate comfort, the long-term consequences can be detrimental.

Temporary discomfort, long-term benefits vs temporary comfort, long-term consequences? The choice is yours.

ACTIVITY 3: Make Your Self-Care Toolkit

Whether you've got folks cheering you on or you're navigating the boundary-setting journey solo, don't wait for external validation. Trust your instincts and take charge. It might feel a bit overwhelming, but this exercise will empower you every step of the way, regardless of whether you have support or not.

- Compile a list of self-care activities that rejuvenate you.
- Write down every small thing you can do to nurture your well-being. Remember to focus more on self-care activities and a few self-indulging ones.
- Ensure those two don't contradict each other. For instance, don't plan to wake up in the morning as a self-care activity and watch late-night TV as self-indulgence. You will burn out, and it won't be sustainable.

All these activities will serve as your go-to resources throughout your boundary-setting journey. You can lean on these activities when you find yourself overwhelmed.

You can find a free self-care toolkit e-book on my website - https://alekhyakoruti.com/say-yes-to-you-landing-page#freedownloads. Download it if you need a few selfcare ideas to get started.

Now, armed with the knowledge of the boundaries you need to work on and equipped with a toolkit of self-care activities, you're ready to tackle the journey, whether on your own or with the support you may have.

Now, let's start with boundary setting in one of the biggest areas of our lives.

*** *** ***

In a Nutshell 52

> Consider the 6 categories of boundaries for a comprehensive approach.
> Encourage an open dialogue with others for better understanding.
> Find your 'why' before you set boundaries so that you maintain them more successfully.
> Prioritize self-care, which is different from self-indulgence, while setting boundaries.
> Build a self-care toolkit to navigate the challenges of boundary setting effectively.

Setting Boundaries in Relationships

"Boundaries are the distance at which I can love you and me simultaneously."

- Prentis Hemphill

4

"If you love somebody, you shouldn't think twice before sacrificing or compromising for them."

We've heard this sentence or similar versions of it way too many times to count right. Yes, healthy relationships do have a factor of all these things, but in a respectful amount.

It is common to see boundaries being violated left, right and centre when it comes to romantic relationships because we don't feel it's necessary to put boundaries for someone we love. Some people I met found it much easier to set boundaries with friends and work, but this area was like an open minefield.

One of the most unfortunate reasons why people don't set boundaries in romantic relationships is because they feel the other person will leave and that they'll end up alone. The fear of being alone or abandoned keeps them in unhealthy relationships where they sacrifice their happiness and well-being to please their partner.

I feel that 'sacrifice' has become a very celebrated word. If you sacrifice, you're a good partner. Not just in romantic relationships, sacrifice equates to selflessness, devotion, and commitment in almost every relationship in life. I'd like to reframe that and swap out 'sacrifice' with the word 'choice'.

Let's shift our perspective to making choices instead of viewing them as a sacrifice. Instead of hiding behind the idea of sacrifice, feeling like a martyr, and being miserable, let's embrace choices. This way, we have control over our decisions, whether they lead to positive or negative outcomes. It's about taking ownership and being okay with the results.

If you find yourself facing a difficult decision—one that might not bring immediate comfort but holds long-term benefits— embrace it. Life seldom dishes out choices that come with instant gratification. Making tough choices might seem hard, but remember, it's your call. You're in charge, and you won't feel like you 'sacrificed' anything.

Making a choice places you in the driver's seat of your life. Sacrificing something, especially when it feels forced rather than chosen, can leave you with a sense of disempowerment, even if it wasn't intentional.

Changing the narrative just a little bit can make you feel empowered, and that is important in boundary setting.

You should feel empowered when you set boundaries, not fear or doubt.

When it comes to relationships, go for boundaries that suit both you and your partner. If you're feeling disrespected or like your voice isn't heard, take a look at your own boundaries. Putting the blame on your partner won't fix things. What works better is making choices that empower you and help build a healthier relationship.

*** *** ***

It is well-established in the psychological literature that setting and maintaining healthy boundaries contribute to improved interpersonal well-being, reduced conflicts, better communication, and enhanced overall relationship satisfaction.

From my time helping some folks out, I've seen a lot of them turn from being sceptics to full-fledged believers in the power of setting boundaries in their relationships. And you know what? They're pretty pleased with themselves for making that choice!

Two such converts were Ayesha and Raghav. They went from having no boundaries and being miserable to setting boundaries and thriving in happy relationships with their respective partners.

Ayesha was the kind of person who would drop everything just to make her partner happy. If he wanted to go out, even after she'd had a super long day, she'd say yes without a second thought. And if he suggested a movie night, she'd jump on it, even if she knew she had to be up early the next day. Her partner loved surprising her with trips, which meant Ayesha had to scramble to get time off work, and it wasn't always easy. But here's the thing – her partner thought she was totally into all of it. He had no clue that it was actually stressing her out.

On the other hand, Raghav had set a few boundaries with his partner. He once communicated the need to rest for an entire day on the weekend because he had a job that required a significant amount of physical exertion, leaving him thoroughly exhausted. Unfortunately, he never communicated it again nor maintained the boundary because he felt that he should please his wife, who was always excited for the weekend and made elaborate plans for them.

In both cases, they didn't communicate or maintain their boundaries, which ended up being detrimental. Ayesha and Raghav liked being 'givers' in the relationship and thought they were making a 'sacrifice' for the sake of the relationship instead of accepting that they just made wrong choices repeatedly. Over time, they got mentally and physically exhausted, resentful towards their spouses, and even had episodes of extreme anger because they never had time to pause and recharge.

Just like everyone, they believed that boundaries would damage their relationship. When they realised that not having healthy boundaries was what was causing a lot of harm, they sat down with their partners and discussed it.

Ayesha and Raghav shared their struggles with their

unsuspecting spouses, who, upon learning about the challenges, immediately supported their boundaries. No complaints or arguments. This honest conversation paved the way for understanding and respect to thrive in their relationships.

So, let me say it once again - Healthy relationships thrive on boundaries.

Before ruling out the idea of setting boundaries, give it a try, even if you think your partner might not fully get it. Don't buy into movie plots that glamorize no boundary setting or clear boundary violations in the name of love, like the whole notion of 'chasing' someone.

How about we celebrate heroes who actually respect boundaries? Sure, it might not make for a thrilling movie, but it's high time we normalize the simple act of setting and respecting each other's boundaries!

Back in 2009, I had this eye-opening conversation with a dear friend that completely flipped my views on relationships. I used to think you should just shower love in a relationship without expecting anything in return. As long as there's love and respect, I figured that's all you need. Probably, I had a very movie-like impression where you just feel happy by being the giver, not expecting anything in return but love.

But here's the gem my friend threw at me: relationships actually need a few expectations. Having zero expectations might sound cool, but there has to be something that makes your partner stand out from your average buddy.

For instance, it's okay to not expect your friend to check on you when you're sick, but your partner? Totally different story. If you keep brushing it off like, "Oh, it's fine if they don't check on me every time I'm sick," it's not fair. You might be okay with it at first, but eventually, you'll wonder why your partner isn't any different from a friend who didn't show up. Resentment might start brewing, and if you don't deal with it, things can go downhill fast.

So, my friend challenged my belief that you shouldn't have expectations. He made me truly believe that having expectations is actually a good thing, but the key is to communicate them. If you don't, you'll end up being a giver, which isn't bad, but what happens when your cup is empty? Having some expectations will ensure that your cup doesn't get too empty.

Anticipating your partner to respect your boundaries is a good expectation. Understanding each other's expectations and being open to communication is vital. Having some flexibility when boundaries get crossed helps keep the relationship stress-free.

It's also important for your partner to expect that you won't flip out if they accidentally cross a flexible boundary. Constant worry about setting you off can stress them out, damaging your relationship.

But here's the deal: You have to be clear about the boundaries that are non-negotiable for you. These are the ones that should never be crossed.

Establishing Non-Negotiables

I recently saw an interesting video on boundaries.

Henry Ammar, a transformation expert, spoke about how he learnt about boundaries from porcupines. He narrated an incident where he saw a bunch of porcupines huddling together on a cold day to keep themselves warm. As soon as they huddled too close, their quills started piercing each other, and they all dispersed. But it was really cold, and they tried huddling again, and the same thing happened. Henry observed the porcupines repeat this 'huddle-disperse' process until they found the sweet spot where none of their quills were hurting each other.

For them, huddling close to keep each other warm was an act of love. However, this love didn't prevent them from getting hurt when they got too close, and their spiky quills poked each other.

This was indeed a great lesson on boundaries! This incident demonstrates that we all need close relationships to thrive and get through life, but getting too close can end up hurting us, even if there's a lot of love. We need to find the right spot from which we can support each other without invading each other's space or hurting each other.

Like Henry, I would have never expected to learn a lesson on boundaries from porcupines, but what a lesson to learn!

Before you can understand where that sweet spot is for you, you need to first identify what your non-negotiables are. Defining these will be your starting point for setting boundaries in relationships.

Why Define Non-Negotiable Boundaries

To understand this, let's look at the famous TV couple that kept the audience on the edge of their seats wondering 'will-they-won't-they,' Ross and Rachel of FRIENDS.

They went through many ups and downs, most of which could have been avoided if they just communicated their non-negotiables and set clear boundaries. Who knows, this could have prevented the whole 'we were on a break' debate altogether. Their relationship took a hit because they had different interpretations of what it meant to 'take a break.' It took them a few years to figure out they still loved each other. After spending too much time apart, they finally got back together.

Non-negotiable boundaries are the foundation of healthy relationships. These are ones that you establish firmly and refuse to budge on. Your non-negotiables will reflect your core values, priorities, and limits. These will communicate what you can tolerate in your relationship and what you won't.

A common example of a non-negotiable for individuals in a strictly monogamous relationship revolves around cheating. Any violation of this boundary may result in the disintegration of the relationship. Of course, addressing such complex matters involves considering multiple layers and factors, which is a topic for another day.

My point is, if you recognize a specific behaviour as a non-negotiable and anticipate it causing distress when violated, communicate it with your partner with confidence. If they still choose to violate it, you may have some thinking to do about where your relationship stands.

Non-negotiables give clear guidelines for both partners, reducing the chances of misunderstandings or conflicts when respected. They offer emotional intimacy by creating a sense of trust and safety, nurturing emotional intimacy.

Setting non-negotiable boundaries is an act of self-respect. It lets your partner know that you value yourself and your well-being. When you assert your boundaries confidently, it will contribute to a positive self-image, too, which will influence all areas of your life.

ACTIVITY 4: List Non-Negotiables

This activity will help you narrow down your non-negotiables in your relationship.

- List out your non-negotiables using pen and paper. Don't make a mental list because you will forget. It's better to write them down clearly.

- An important thing to remember while doing this activity is to focus on YOUR feelings, not others. No, it's not a selfish thing to do. If you still think that way, now would be a good time to chuck that idea out of your head once and for all. Remember, focusing on your well-being is never selfish.

- Depending on how aligned and clear you are about your values and priorities, this step may take you a few minutes or a few days. Either is fine, just don't rush.

Now that you are clear on what boundaries you want to set in your relationship, you need to learn how to recognise boundary violations, both intentional and unintentional.

If it's unintentional, reach out to our partner and convey the same and communicate clearly what they could do instead. Discuss and reach a solution that works for both of you.

If it's intentional, you may have to take the call on how you want to proceed with the relationship, especially if the boundary violation is a repeating pattern.

Recognizing Boundary Violations

There is absolutely no one on this planet who would never violate someone's boundary. Even the most well-intentioned, well-meaning, and loving person can cross or violate a boundary unknowingly. But before you can convey it to them, you need to learn to identify boundary violations. Boundary violations can manifest in different ways, and these are the signs you need to keep an eye out for.

Some signs of boundary violations in relationships include disrespect, abuse, neglecting your needs and feelings, and invading your personal space. Tune into your feelings and emotions to see if you feel discomfort, hurt, anger, sadness, or resentment.

Now, you may say it's normal to feel these emotions even when boundaries aren't violated. I agree. Those feelings are not exclusive to boundary violations. But it could be one of the reasons. Only you can differentiate and understand if that negative emotion was because of a boundary violation or something else.

I'm just giving you tricks and tools to make this journey easier. If you are in the most healthy, loving relationship and feel this chapter isn't for you, great! But it's always better to know these things. Who knows, maybe you can identify these signs in a loved one who may be in a bad place and help them instead.

Boundary violations tend to leave a heavy emotional toll on the person whose boundaries are being crossed. The psychological and emotional impact of boundary violation can lead to eroded trust, strained relationships, helplessness, anxiety, a sense of powerlessness, or lack of control over your own life. In severe cases, it can even cause depression or mental trauma, for which they may need professional help.

So, if you know your non-negotiables and communicate them well and in a respectful manner, you will avoid all this. When you are clear about your why, you can convey the reason behind setting that particular boundary clearly. If you aren't clear, then you will be vague while communicating. This means the boundary won't be clear or taken seriously, and it will not hold.

"But how do I tell them?" I know, I know. It isn't lost on me that communicating boundaries to your partner can be tricky, especially when you have never done it before. But this is what the book will help you with.

Communicating Your Boundaries

Sinduja was always a little overweight due to a medical condition. It made her feel really conscious, but she tried her best to stay as healthy and fit as she could. Over time, she learned to accept her size and was perfectly at peace with it.

Until she started dating Arun, whom she had known since college. Since they had been friends for years and always pulled each other's legs, he didn't think too much when he would make a joke or two about her size. But it had started affecting Sinduja a lot.

In fact, she was surprised that he would joke about it because he was aware of her insecurity about her size. Because she didn't want to be seen as a sensitive girlfriend, she didn't voice out her disappointment and kept it to herself. But one fine day, it culminated in a huge fight that started from a very petty and tiny thing.

That's when she realised that Arun didn't even know that it was hurting her, mainly because she always laughed along and took a jab at him too. He genuinely thought it was just playful banter. Once she communicated that it really bothered and hurt her, Arun apologised and never repeated it again. In fact, he even stepped in when someone was making a joke about her size when she wasn't around.

That's the power of communication.

If someone truly loves you, they will not intentionally do things that will hurt you. But you need to let them know. Jokes and playful banter can be interpreted differently by different people, so it's always a good idea to immediately let your partner know if a joke hurts you. They will respect your boundaries because they love and care about you. Unless someone is intentionally making hurtful comments out of spite, they will respect your boundaries.

We have made up our minds, thanks to overthinking, that talking to them will be awkward or damaging or whatever it is that your little voice convinces you of. Get it out of your mind! Nobody will think anything!

The key is to communicate politely yet firmly and assertively.

"But I'm a naturally shy person. What should I do?"

This next segment will help you.

The Role of Assertive and Respectful Communication

You need to effectively communicate your needs, desires, and limits clearly and assertively for successful boundary setting.

No one will take you seriously if you convey your boundaries with doubt or fear. They will probably just brush it off and carry on doing what they always did.

On the other hand, if you say it rudely or harshly, it can impact your relationship.

You have to find the balance between aggression and passivity. Be firm yet polite, kind but assertive.

The tonality of your voice will make all the difference here, and I must say, it isn't always easy.

I had such a tough time finding this balance. I constantly swayed between the two, and it took a lot of work to get to where I got. Honestly, I'm still working on it because we can always do better here.

Speaking assertively and with politeness fosters an open and honest dialogue with your partner, cultivating an environment of mutual respect and consideration. It's a space where you advocate for your boundaries without encroaching on or violating others' personal space. It's about setting your limits without overstepping theirs.

Assertive communication is a skill, which means even if you struggle with it, you can learn it. If you are comfortable and good at it, you can refine it further, This skill empowers you to navigate personal relationships with grace and confidence, ensuring that your boundaries are heard and respected.

You just need some tools and techniques in your kitty to master this skill and I'll share the ones that will help you.

One of the biggest tools in the bag of assertive communication is the "I" statement.

The Power of "I" Statements

When I first came to know about 'I' statements, the technique kind of felt silly. It sounded too simple a tactic to even work.

Let me tell you, it does work. "I" statements are so powerful that they can single-handedly diffuse a tense situation.

I honestly wondered why we aren't taught these tools for healthy communication regardless and not as something to learn only when things go bad. I went back to a couple of conflicts I recently had with my husband and realised how this one tool could have mitigated them.

"I" statements, as the name clearly suggests, allow you to express your needs, feelings, and expectations without putting the blame on the other person or accusing them.

It seems pretty easy and straightforward, but if you're not used to it, it could take you a little while to get the hang of it. Once you do, though, it becomes like second nature, and things tend to go pretty smoothly with fewer conflicts.

The mistake I would make earlier was that I would express my feelings and needs and highlight my expectations, but suffixed and prefixed those statements by placing the blame nicely on my poor husband.

"I" statements also help the other person understand your feelings better and respond more positively without getting defensive or upset.

Which one do you think will work –

"I need to set this boundary because 'you' do this, and it stressed me out."

Or,

"I need this boundary because it helps 'me' feel calmer."

The first one places blame, and the second one focuses on you and how they can help you.

Your loved ones will help or support you in any way they can if you just ask them. So, don't be afraid to speak up.

Here are some examples of "I" statements to get you started.

Situation	Non-I Statement (Blaming)	'I' Statement (Expressing Boundaries)
Partner neglecting your needs	"You never listen to me."	"I feel unheard when my requests go unacknowledged."
Overwhelming family requests	"You always expect too much."	"I need some space. I'm feeling really overwhelmed with so many requests."
Invasion of personal space	"You invade my privacy all the time."	"I don't feel comfortable when my personal space isn't respected."
Disagreeing on household chores	"You're lazy and never help."	"I'd like us to discuss a fair distribution of chores."
Constant criticism from a friend	"You're so critical all the time."	"I feel hurt when I receive frequent criticism."
Partner not respecting boundaries	"You're so insensitive."	"I feel hurt when my boundaries aren't respected."
Pressure to socialize	"You make me do things I hate."	"I'd prefer to have some alone time tonight."

Invasion of work-life balance	"You never give me space to work."	"I need to focus on work right now; can we please talk later?"

The thing is, these seem quite easy to use, but you may not be able to instantly think of such statements in real time, especially when you're new to this technique.

You can change that with the next tool.

Boundary Scripts

You know what I absolutely hate. When you have a disagreement or argument with someone, and you try to make your point, and your brain just goes on strike. It just blanks out, and no matter how hard you think, nothing good comes to your mind.

And then days later, in some cases even years later, when you're doing something absolutely random, the best comeback response pops into your mind, and you almost beat yourself up for not being able to think of it during the argument.

Then you spend days, weeks, and months replaying that incident in your mind and imagining you saying that perfect comeback during the actual argument and how things would have been different because of that.

Imagine that happening when you're trying to set boundaries. You're attempting to establish boundaries, you're already nervous and then your brain decides to shut down.

So, instead of being kind and firm, you end up being aggressive. Despite knowing that you need to use the "I" statements, you end up blaming the other person. As a result, the boundaries never get set because it becomes too emotional or intense.

You do not want that happening!

Boundary scripts are excellent in preparing you to give

appropriate responses. They are basically scripted phrases that you prepare ahead of time that clearly express your limits, expectations, and needs.

By incorporating boundary scripts into your communication arsenal, you empower yourself to express your boundaries clearly and assertively.

Don't go unprepared into a situation where you might have to set a boundary, hoping words will magically flow. More often than not, the opposite will happen. Before discussing something serious, you may prepare mentally and think you're confident, but when the moment comes, you might blank out, say something different, or avoid the topic due to sheer awkwardness or lack of confidence.

Boundary scripts can be your secret weapon that can help you convey exactly what you want in a clear manner without fumbling or feeling underconfident.

Now, if you think this is a silly thing to stand in front of a mirror and practice scripts, think about it this way - you always prepare beforehand for a difficult situation like an exam or an important presentation. This is about your well-being, so why feel awkward to prepare beforehand and tackle the situation with confidence instead of awkwardness, guilt, fear, or shame.

There is nothing wrong if you need to work on your confidence. Even if you are confident and know exactly what to say, there's no harm in running down the scenario once before it actually happens.

Here are some examples of boundary scripts:

- Boundary Script 1: "I need some alone time to recharge. I would love to schedule some 'me time' when we don't have any urgent plans."

- Boundary Script 2: "I value our relationship, and I'd like us to communicate openly and honestly. Can we decide upon a time that works for us to discuss this?

- Boundary Script 3: "It's important for me to feel respected. I would like it if we could watch our tone and avoid yelling during disagreements."

ACTIVITY 5: Write Boundary Scripts Based on Non-Negotiables

It's time to make your boundary scripts and work on your confidence.

- Bring out your list of non-negotiables and boundaries that you need to set in your relationship. You can include boundaries related to communication, personal space, respect, or your emotional needs.

- Craft your scripts. Write down phrases that will help you communicate your boundaries clearly, politely, yet assertively. Remember that your scripted phrases need to be respectful to the other person.

- Anticipate different reactions you might get and prepare scripts for them as well. Be willing to modify the scripts if the circumstances change or your flexibility with the boundary changes.

- Ensure your scripts reflect your evolving needs.

You have to consider the possibility of your partner not responding positively immediately to your boundaries. If they need time, be willing to give them instead of forcing your boundaries at that very instant.

Just like you probably took time to understand which boundaries you needed and practiced your scripts, it's only fair to give them the time, if they need it, to get on the same page as you.

Ask them if they need any more clarity, communicate more, and be open to answering their questions if they are genuinely curious.

ACTIVITY 6: Role-Play

(We'll revisit this activity with the same set of instructions in the upcoming chapters.)

Your scripts serve as a roadmap for navigating challenging conversations and maintaining healthy, respectful relationships. They allow you to communicate your boundaries in a non-confrontational manner.

Your job doesn't end by just writing them out once. You need to engage in some role-play exercises with a trusted friend, relative, or your boundary buddies. Here's how you do it.

- Choose a specific scenario that you'd like to address and set a boundary in.

- Assign someone the role of your partner to bounce off the script with. You can also switch roles where you can assume the role of your partner because you may anticipate their needs better and observe how your role-play partner responds. You may even get a few ideas that you may want to incorporate.

- Focus on delivering the script that you prepared confidently and assertively. Ask your boundary buddy how well these factors were showing or if you need to work further on them.

- Take feedback from your boundary buddy and analyse if anything went wrong and how you can improve it.

- Practice till you feel confident to have the actual conversation with your partner.

- Repeat with other scenarios if needed.

Make sure you practice in a low-pressure environment. This is very important.

When you practice enough times without pressure, you will gain confidence and be prepared to do the same in an emotionally charged or high-pressure environment.

If you don't have a boundary buddy, stand in front of the mirror with a picture of your partner taped. Do whatever works for you, but don't skip practicing; otherwise, the point of making boundary scripts will be lost.

It may be hard to associate 'practice' with boundary setting, but it is absolutely essential to master this skill. Communication is a skill, and just like any other skill, it needs practice, and the more you practice, the better you get and the more confidence you gain.

Hopefully, you're feeling slightly more confident about setting healthy boundaries in relations? Now, let's tackle the area where you spend most of your waking hours.

*** *** ***

In a Nutshell

> Healthy boundaries strengthen romantic relationships.
> Replacing the word 'sacrifice' with 'choice' can help you make better relationship and boundaries decisions.
> Place some expectations from your relationship.
> The flexibility of boundaries will evolve as the relationship evolves.
> Identify your non-negotiable and use them to set healthy relationship boundaries.
> Learning to recognize boundary violations is as important as setting them.

> Use "I" statements and practice boundary scripts for successful boundary setting.

Boundary Setting at Work

"Your ability to set clear boundaries directly correlates with your success and well-being in the workplace." –

Oprah Winfrey

5

How much time do you spend at work?

The average person spends over a third of their life at the workplace. A lot of us are guilty of even stretching that number to a few extra years because we are so consumed by work. This could be because you genuinely love what you do and spend all your waking hours doing the work, or you don't know how to put boundaries at work.

The sad truth is that most of us don't have a clear delineation between work and personal life. The hustle culture these days glorifies overworking, sleeping less, and not having a personal life because apparently work is everything. Being 'busy' is a tag that many wear with so much pride that it isn't even warranted.

Let's try to view work just as a part of life and not make it our entire identity.

And this can begin with healthy and firm boundary setting.

I didn't even have to look beyond my home to understand the repercussions of poor boundary setting at work. Violations of work boundaries within our house caused way too many conflicts than we would like to admit!

My husband used to love what he did. He woke up with so much excitement each day about what he did and spoke about his work with so much passion. I loved that about him.

One fine day, it all changed because he didn't know how to set work boundaries. Even when he tried, he wasn't consistent or firm about maintaining them, which essentially gave others the freedom to violate his boundaries as they wished. And because he didn't know how to say no at work, our relationship took a few hits.

He would receive calls at 3am or at odd hours when we were fast asleep or busy with personal work on a holiday to answer a seemingly urgent question. He worked almost all the weekends and festivals, leaving me alone on most of our free days. I lost count of the number of times he had to dress up and leave in the middle of his day off because they requested his presence 'urgently', and he didn't know how to say no.

We've had conversations lasting days about how he should hold stronger boundaries, and he never could because he felt it was his responsibility to be a team player. Well, it's difficult to be a team player when you're the only one showing up constantly, and others don't.

During international vacations, I anticipated that he would still receive calls. Since we couldn't leave his phone behind, I opted for the next best solution to give him a break from work calls. I would take the local SIM card, rendering his phone inactive, and the only time he could connect to Wi-Fi was back at the hotel at the end of the day. Which is when his phone would buzz nonstop for 15 minutes with work notifications.

Resorting to such extreme measures was the only way to ensure some uninterrupted quality time with him. Even at home, there were occasions when I had to hide his phone because it incessantly rang or pinged, consuming a significant portion of his day off.

I'm very sure this isn't a standalone story. I had a colleague who was always available at all hours, all days of the week, irrespective of whether she was working or on leave. One day, she didn't pick up the phone, and people got worried. Turns out it was her day off, and her husband did what I did - hid her phone and forced her to spend uninterrupted time with him for just one day!

That's really not how it should be right. No wonder people are so burnt out and exhausted, and some are even quitting corporate life because it's no longer appealing. It's just too demanding, with absolutely no room for personal lives.

Many of you may find yourselves living a similar narrative or know someone who does. If you've skipped social events, family functions, or trips with friends, just for work, you aren't alone. It's a common struggle that often leaves us questioning the balance between our personal lives and professional commitments.

Not everyone has the luxury of being able to quit, move to something less demanding, or start something of their own. So, does that mean we have to continue to struggle with work-life constantly seeping into our personal lives?

Not really.

While achieving work-life balance may seem challenging, there are certain steps we can take to make it a bit more possible.

I understand that workplace can be a really tricky place to set boundaries because of multiple reasons. Your paycheck is in the hands of someone else, you don't want to be thought of as someone who isn't a team player (like my husband), or you don't want to risk an appraisal.

But if you don't want to burn out and still enjoy what you do for many years to come, start setting some boundaries. Start by following the 'comfort expansion' idea that we discussed in Chapter 2.

Start with just one small, doable boundary and stick to it. Then do another and repeat. Don't take a huge step and put multiple unrealistic boundaries at the same time. That is a recipe for failure, and you will give up before you even start.

This chapter will show you how to set boundaries in this tricky area without negative repercussions on your professional life but benefit your personal life.

Work-Life Balance Audit

One of the most famous movies from which we can learn about the importance of setting boundaries is 'The Devil Wears Prada'. Anne's character, Andrea, was at the beck and call of her boss, sabotaging her relationship and friendship with colleagues.

Her personal life suffered too. She had absolutely no work boundaries, and once she realised what it all had cost her, she quit the job, tried to repair things, and had some sense of balance. Since it was a movie, it all worked out for her in the end; we can't say the same about real life.

Working professionals desire work-life balance so much that almost every company advertises itself as a big believer in the same, especially to attract new hires. Once the last leg of hiring is completed, it's a whole different story. It's like you went in and sat in a different movie than what you bought the ticket for.

To be fair, we can't really achieve a perfect work-life balance. It isn't possible to have a balanced life every single day. There will be days when your work needs you more and days when your personal life needs you more. As long as you are focusing on both, it's fine.

The problem arises when there is a complete disregard for personal life and the people in it. Expecting family and friends to understand every single time work takes precedence isn't fair.

There is enough research done to study this, and they all say that individuals who maintain a healthy balance between their work and personal lives experience lower stress levels, improved mental health, and more meaningful relationships. They are more productive and creative in their professional lives too.

So, while it may not be possible to switch gears and achieve the perfect work-life balance right from day one, we can at least identify how imbalanced it is by doing a quick work-life balance audit.

Use this detailed point system to assess your work-life balance, and the final score will provide you with a more nuanced understanding of your current situation.

Score yourself on a scale of 1-5, 1 if the statement almost never applies to 5 when it applies most of the time.

Work Hours

- Do you regularly work more than the standard hours expected from your job?
- Are you frequently asked to work overtime or take work home?

Leisure Time

- Do you find it challenging to set aside time for hobbies, interests, or relaxation?
- Have you missed out on social events or gatherings due to work commitments?

Physical Health

- Are you experiencing physical symptoms of stress, such as headaches, fatigue, or muscle tension?
- Do you have time for regular exercise and a balanced diet?

Mental Health

- Have you felt overwhelmed, anxious, or mentally exhausted because of work-related stress?
- Do you regularly take breaks to clear your mind during the workday?

Relationships

- Have your relationships with family or friends been strained due to work demands?
- Do you have quality time for your loved ones without work distractions?

Vacation and Time-Off

- Have you been hesitant to take vacations or time off work due to workload concerns?
- When you do take time off, do you find it hard to fully disconnect from work?

Boundaries

- Do you often check work emails or messages during non-working hours?
- Are you expected to be available for work-related matters 24/7?

Personal Goals

- Have you had to delay or abandon personal goals or aspirations because of work demands?
- Do you have a clear sense of your personal and professional priorities?

Stress Coping Strategies

- Are you relying on unhealthy coping mechanisms like excessive caffeine, alcohol, or other substances?
- Do you have healthy stress management techniques in place, such as meditation or mindfulness?

Overall Satisfaction

- On a scale of 1-10, how satisfied are you with your current work-life balance?

Scoring:

Add up the points for each statement to calculate your final score and check where you stand.

10-25: Excellent Work-Life Balance
26-40: Good Work-Life Balance
41-60: Moderate Work-Life Balance
61-80: Fair Work-Life Balance
81-100: Poor Work-Life Balance

Use your responses to pinpoint areas that need adjustment. If you scored very poorly in some areas, maybe that's where you need to set a boundary first.

Common Signs of Work-Life Imbalance

Hrithik Roshan's character Arjun in Zindagi Na Milegi Dobara was another great reel example I've seen of someone with horrible work boundaries.

His best friend planned a wonderful trip to Spain, which Arjun was initially reluctant to even go for as he did not want to miss work. (Who thinks twice about a trip like that!) During the trip, he kept working and even stopped in the middle of nowhere to attend a work call. He couldn't truly enjoy the trip on certain occasions because he was working and expected his friends, whom he met after years, to understand that he couldn't take a break for even a few days.

While it is easy to judge his character and say it was silly of him to work on that trip, many of us are absolutely guilty of that! Maybe we didn't hop on a video call in the middle of nowhere, but we have answered emails, messages, and calls during non-working hours, especially on holidays. We couldn't push the pause button for a few days. I know I've done it too many times to count.

We may come up with a million reasons to justify it; we know it isn't right, but we do it anyway.

I've worked in buses, cabs, and flights. I've even worked in the middle of my friends' weddings, locked in a room listening to fun songs everyone was dancing to just a few feet away. I even found myself attending to a seemingly important call 3 minutes before I had to sit for my exam because, apparently, putting up an Instagram post was more important than me sitting for an exam!

I kept insisting that I couldn't do it as I had an exam in exactly 2 minutes, and he kept insisting that it would just take a minute. He wanted me to make some changes and send it right away because they had to post it immediately. That I was 'allowed' to sit for my exam only after I did that! It didn't take a minute, it took 10! I started the exam late, with a stressed-out and frenzied mind. And guess what? The post never went live till after my exam was finished.

I took a long, hard look at my work boundaries that day and realised I needed to set much stronger work boundaries. I was displaying all the signs of work-life imbalance, and I knew I had to make a few changes quickly.

I just thought these signs were a result of working hard and for long hours. It never crossed my mind that it could actually indicate work-life imbalance. Check if you have these too:

1. Constant Fatigue: Feeling consistently tired or drained, even after a full night's sleep.
2. Lack of Personal Time: Struggling to find time for personal activities, hobbies, or relaxation.
3. Poor Physical Health: Experiencing frequent health issues or a decline in overall well-being due to stress or overwork.
4. Strained Relationships: Difficulties in maintaining healthy relationships with family and friends due to time constraints or emotional exhaustion.
5. Decreased Productivity: A decline in job performance and efficiency due to mental or physical fatigue.
6. Neglecting Self-Care: Ignoring basic self-care needs such as exercise, proper nutrition, or sufficient sleep.
7. Feeling Overwhelmed: Constantly feeling overwhelmed by work demands and unable to find a healthy work-life

balance.

8. Difficulty Concentrating: Struggling to concentrate or stay focused on tasks due to mental exhaustion.
9. Neglected Hobbies: No longer engaging in activities that once brought joy or relaxation.
10. Increased Stress and Anxiety: Experiencing heightened levels of stress and anxiety related to work pressures and demands.

I was lucky, as a thriving freelancer, to be in a position to quit working for those clients and choose someone else. I understand not everyone can do the same despite wanting to, but you can start by setting work boundaries in the existing workplace.

It's always a good idea to have healthy work boundaries, even if you don't have any of these signs right now or if you absolutely love your job. You do not want to reach a stage where you start hating the job you once absolutely loved (like what happened with my husband).

Take a page out of these inspirational tycoons and aim to get some level of balance in your life.

Richard Branson, the founder of the Virgin Group, encourages his employees to maintain a healthy work-life balance. He is known for his adventurous lifestyle and emphasizes the importance of enjoying life outside of work.

Arianna Huffington, the co-founder of The Huffington Post, is a vocal advocate for work-life balance. After collapsing from exhaustion in 2007, she became an advocate for sleep and prioritizing well-being. She says, "Boundaries are the space where you can be your most authentic self at work. When you honour your own boundaries, you invite others to do the same."

Sheryl Sandberg, the COO of Facebook, promotes the idea of integrating work and life rather than trying to balance them separately. She encourages a flexible approach to work hours and emphasizes the importance of quality time with family. This is what she has to say - "Your work should not define your worth. Setting boundaries at work is a way of valuing yourself beyond your professional role."

Oprah Winfrey, the media mogul and philanthropist, has stressed the significance of finding a balance between work and personal life. She values downtime, self-reflection, and maintaining a healthy lifestyle.

Tony Robbins, a hugely popular motivational speaker, says, "In the fast-paced world of work, boundaries are your anchor. They keep you grounded, focused, and ultimately more successful."

If you want to take a step towards having a balanced life but don't know how to navigate, try the next tool.

The Traffic Light System

"Setting boundaries is a crucial skill in any professional's toolbox. It not only preserves your sanity but also enhances your effectiveness." – Brené Brown

You probably cross a dozen traffic light signals on the way to work and never would have thought that the same system could be applied to set up boundaries at work.

The Traffic Light Boundary System, also known as the 'Red-Amber-Green' System, is a visual representation to set work boundaries, which was devised by Hodology – a leadership coaching company.

Just like the traffic light tells the drivers on the road what exactly to do based on the lights and conveys what is permissible, this system can be used to convey what's permissible and off-limits for you when it comes to work.

Let's see how to use it in the context of boundary setting.

Red Boundary (Firm, Inflexible)

These are your work non-negotiables. Any task, action or behaviour that is unacceptable to you, categorise them as red boundaries. It can also represent conversations that are off-limits for you at work.

A common red boundary is family time or leaving work at a particular time every day because you need to pick up your kid from school.

When I came across this system, a fellow MBA peer instantly came to mind. I had never met or seen her, but I heard her once in the online sessions where she spoke about having a firm rule of not attending any calls on weekends or holidays because it was strictly family time. She stuck to that boundary extremely well.

She spoke about how she was viewed as someone stubborn and inflexible, but she held her ground. She had made that boundary clear when she interviewed for the job and reminded her peers and superiors of the same when they complained about this rule.

When asked if it was harsh on her to hear people always crib about it, she simply said, "I know my priorities and I refuse to budge for people who don't priorities themselves or their families. That's their choice. This is mine. When I'm at work, they get my 100%, and I don't get distracted by home. When at home, I want to give my 100% to my family and not get distracted by work. They can work without me for 2 days of the week or holidays. If they can't, they need to rethink how qualified people within the team actually are."

Over time, people understood that she was serious about this boundary and stopped bothering her when she wasn't working.

I wished I was like her. I wish a lot of us were like her. I don't remember your name, dear MBA peer, but if you are reading this, please know that what you said really inspired me to set stricter work boundaries, which I did.

Amber Boundaries (Semi-flexible)

These indicate boundaries where you can have a certain level of flexibility. These boundaries are negotiable or may have exceptions. You are willing to bend these boundaries once in a while, but not every time.

Amber boundaries could be reserved for occasions where there is immense work pressure, and everyone is needed to chip in by working extra. But 'limit' is key here. When the opportunities align with your personal and team goals, you can put tasks under these boundaries.

It's easy to slip from yellow boundaries to having no boundaries. If you don't stick to flexibility limits, no one will take your boundaries seriously, and you will be expected to work all the time.

This is what happened with my husband. He was fine with taking on an extra day or two of work by giving up his holiday, but he didn't make it clear how many times was too many times. Eventually, it ended up being a complete violation of boundaries because he always gave in.

As family, I knew that certain critical situations would arise where his presence would be needed without fail. I completely respected that and consistently supported him during genuine emergencies. However, there were instances when it was clear that they could have managed without him but still called him on his day off. It was frustrating to be patient when it happened every single time.

Green Boundaries (Completely Flexible and Permissible)

These are actions, behaviours or conversations that are permissible without any restrictions.

These include being open to any social interaction that's pertaining to work, taking a break with your work friends when it doesn't interrupt your work, or receiving feedback. You can accommodate or even welcome these things in your workday without feeling overextended.

Now, let's see how to implement the Traffic Light Boundary System in your work.

ACTIVITY 7: Make Your Traffic Light System

List all your current and upcoming work commitments, and categorise them in your own Traffic Light system.

Assess your comfort level with each of them and identify which aligns with your career goals and which are in disharmony with personal goals.

Comfort Level (1-5):

Rate your comfort level with each work commitment on a scale of 1 to 5, where 1 is highly uncomfortable and 5 is very comfortable.

Take this as an example.

Work Commitment	Traffic Light Category	Comfort Level (1-5)	Comments/Notes

Task 1	Red (Stop) E.g.: Overtime work without prior notice	2	High stress; need to discuss boundaries. Discuss why sudden, excessive overtime can be detrimental to well-being and how to communicate that it's unacceptable.
Task 2	Yellow (Proceed with Caution) E.g.: Participating in occasional weekend projects	3	Occasional flexibility is required.
Task 3	Green (Go) E.g.: Regular team meetings during business hours	5	Comfortable and aligned with goals.

The tasks in red indicate work commitments that are causing you stress and require immediate attention and boundary setting.

Amber tasks are those that may need a check on flexibility limits. The important thing to remember with amber boundaries is to maintain them strictly. Do not budge over your flexibility limit; otherwise, it will turn into a boundary violation pretty soon.

Green tasks are those that align perfectly well with your work-life balance and that you can maintain comfortably.

Sit with your manager to discuss some of your red boundaries. Barring urgent instances, chances are high that your manager will accommodate your red boundaries or at least agree to figure out a way that will work for both of you. We make the mistake of not even trying to discuss it.

I know of an acquaintance who told her manager that she needed to get back home at 5.30pm every day, at any cost. That was the time her kid got back from preschool, and because she didn't have help at home, she needed to be home when the kid arrived. She offered to work from 7 to 9 pm to make up for leaving early and finishing the day's work. Well, her manager happily obliged.

She was even happy to extend her working hours on days when it was required. Since she was allowed to be home at the time she wanted, she felt less stressed, was happier, and performed even better.

In order for the traffic light system to work in your favour, you need to keep a few things in mind while implementing it and communicating the boundaries to your superiors.

To Set Red Boundaries

- Explain why you need to set this red boundary and convey it very clearly.
- Communicate assertively about which tasks actions, or behaviours are not acceptable to you.
- Give honest reasons and offer alternatives and strategies that are acceptable at the workplace to accommodate your red boundary.

To Negotiate Yellow Boundaries

- Open and honest communication is the key to negotiating yellow boundaries.
- Communicate the frequency or duration of the task that you are willing to be flexible for.

For instance, one weekend or holiday a month, two instances of overtime a month, and so on.

- If possible, try to document, probably over an email detailing the agreement, so that there is no misunderstanding later on.

To Maintain Green Boundaries

- Ensure the green boundaries align with your career growth as well as personal well-being.
- Regularly assess that your green boundaries are consistent and aligned over the course of time with your goals.
- Reinforce green boundaries by regularly communicating your expectations to your colleagues and supervisors.

I've mentioned 'maintaining boundaries' quite a few times up until now. But what does that mean?

Maintain Your Boundaries

Maintaining boundaries is nothing but sticking to the boundaries you've set without exceptions. If you don't maintain the boundaries, people will forget about them over time, and you will find yourself in a stressful state again. When you maintain the boundaries, eventually, your colleagues will get on the same page as you and respect the boundaries you set.

However, maintaining boundaries in a work setting can be very tricky. Not only is communicating these boundaries a challenging task but constantly making others aware of your boundaries can be tiring. It can also impact your work relationship, which isn't ideal since you spend most of your waking hours with these people.

So, how can you maintain work boundaries? One of the most tactical and effective approaches is to kindly reinforce and uphold the work boundaries at the very moment someone is testing or pushing them.

For instance, if someone is constantly calling or messaging you after work hours for some non-essential, non-urgent work, gently tell them you'll get to it tomorrow and that you don't like answering work calls beyond office hours.

Or, when someone is speaking disrespectfully or derogatorily, you can let them know immediately.

Or when called in to work one weekend, you immediately convey that you are willing to do so just this weekend because it's essential and remind them that it is an exception and not the rule that you will work every weekend.

I can almost hear you thinking that it's better to keep quiet and not get into all this at all. Setting boundaries at work can be a bit like walking a tightrope. You want to be assertive without being aggressive and accommodating without being a pushover.

This next section explores the delicate art of negotiating boundaries in a professional setting.

Understanding Boundary Flexibility

Imagine a scenario where a project has the potential to significantly propel your career forward, but it entails putting in extra hours for a period of three months. Now, you've always had a strict boundary against overtime. However, considering the substantial impact on your career advancement, you decide to temporarily adjust this boundary, making an exception for just those three months. Only those three months until the project is over and not beyond that.

This is called boundary flexibility.

Boundary flexibility is an important skill that will help you communicate and negotiate critical workplace boundaries. It refers to your ability to adapt and adjust to professional and personal boundaries based on specific needs and situations.

We all know that workplace emergencies are a real thing. You will need to finish a project on a new deadline, the client may ask for an impromptu presentation of the project, or something major where your presence will be needed. You know what I'm talking about.

This is where boundary flexibility comes in. There could be situations where you just cannot hang on to even your red work boundaries but have to be flexible. Sometimes, you may have to turn your red boundary to amber. But this does not imply that you completely disregard your boundaries, which would be a boundary violation on your end. It's about adopting a conscious and strategic approach to adapting to such situations as needed.

So, what's the difference between boundary flexibility and boundary violation?

The main difference between boundary flexibility and boundary violation is that the former involves making intentional adjustments to your boundaries for the greater good of the team/organization without compromising on your core values and priorities. You are making a conscious choice and approaching the whole situation with a strategic approach. It's your ability to adapt your work boundaries based on the context and for mutual benefit.

On the other hand, boundary violation is when you feel really pressured or coerced to compromise your boundaries against your will or values. It often has a negative effect on your well-being, and boundary violations tend to be unplanned and repeated often.

For instance, boundary flexibility is accommodating a request to work extra for a month because you know it's needed. And you accommodate that request for just that month and not beyond that time frame.

Boundary violation is when you are threatened with getting fired, getting a pay cut, or being held back at work if you don't show up.

In the former, you will be happy to adjust even your red boundary for a month. In the case of the latter, you will show up against your will because of the negative consequences.

It's not about constantly accommodating other's needs. It's about finding a way to thrive in your career without neglecting your needs, limits, and priorities in the long run and respecting company goals as well.

You don't just need boundary flexibility to protect your well-being, but also to leverage it as an asset for career advancement. If an opportunity that's excellent for propelling your career presents itself, boundary flexibility will allow you to stretch your limits instead of being rigid.

Mastering this skill will allow you to approach work boundaries with professionalism, confidence, and success.

It may not be easy. But it's not impossible either.

Repeating Activity: Role-Play

Here are some common workplace scenarios that you may encounter. Just like we did boundary scripts for relationships, you can make assertive yet polite scripts for the workplace so that when the time comes, or you find yourself in such a situation, you are prepared to respond confidently.

Practice assertive communication techniques to find a solution that respects your boundaries while achieving your professional goals. Here are some scenarios that you can write the scripts for:

- Salary Negotiation
- Managing personal time
- Dealing with overtime
- Discussing remote work boundaries
- Client and colleague boundaries
- Negotiating flexibility
- Dealing with pressure to overcommit

We will cover different styles and examples of communication strategies in chapters 7 and 8, which you can use to design your boundary scripts.

You don't have to do it alone. Reach out to your mentors, supervisors, and HR team if you need support. In most cases, they will accommodate or find an alternative that works for everyone. If you don't ask, the answer will always be no. Just take that step to discuss and take it ahead from there.

The workplace is very dynamic, and this area of your life may need more or constant revisions when it comes to boundaries compared to other areas. You may have to adapt and move around the red, yellow, and green activities. So, make sure you regularly assess your work boundaries and make adjustments that help you further in your career but also maintain your personal well-being.

When your work boundaries are being repeatedly violated, and you are feeling extremely stressed, anxious, and burnt out, you need to evaluate what the next best steps are for you. Based on the circumstances of your life, you can either choose to move to something better or stick it out here because of personal reasons. You are the best person to evaluate your situation and come to a decision, but it is always a good idea to be aware of these things. If not at the current workplace, you can adopt these in the next workplace.

Like I had the opportunity to quit and move on, a colleague unfortunately didn't. He worked in a place that made him absolutely miserable, and he never learned how to set effective boundaries. He finally quit after years of being miserable. He didn't find a job immediately but he had reached a point where he felt like having no job was better than having the job he had.

I sincerely hope you don't find yourself in that situation.

You do what's best for you in the current scenario, but being aware will help you approach this aspect of life confidently and strategically.

We've covered setting boundaries in personal life, relationships, and the workplace. We are now heading to an area where people don't even try to set boundaries and then face the absolute worst conflicts compared to all areas.

*** *** ***

In a Nutshell

> Be aware of signs of work-life imbalance
> Implement the Traffic Light System by categorizing your work boundaries into red (non-negotiable), amber (flexible with limits), and green (completely flexible).
> Regularly assess your work-life balance using a point system to identify areas that need adjustment and prioritize aspects crucial for overall well-being.
> Understand when to be flexible with boundaries for the greater good, adapting strategically to workplace demands without compromising core values.
> Consistently reinforce and uphold your set boundaries to ensure they are respected, fostering a healthy work-life balance over the long term.

96

Navigating Family Boundaries

"Setting boundaries within your family is an act of love, not rejection."

– Anonymous

6

How many of you know one or more of these people in your family?

Someone who can't stop lending money because the person asking to borrow is family.

The wife, who works all day in the office, comes back home tired and still gets all the housework done single-handedly at the cost of her well-being because she can't say no or ask for help.

The cousin who lets their sibling get away with anything, no matter what their age is, because they can't say no to their siblings.

The mother who is burnt out beyond belief but still doesn't ask for help because she's not aware of boundary setting.

And there are many more versions of these people in every single family. You probably mentally named the family member who fits these categories.

They can be someone who could have the perfect boundaries in every aspect of their lives, but when it comes to saying no to family, they just can't get around it.

It's true that setting boundaries in families can be very tricky. Setting boundaries, especially in a collectivist culture like India, poses unique challenges.

Though we discussed this at length in Chapter 1, let's do a quick recap.

This type of society places a huge emphasis on close-knit family and community ties. We have strong cultural norms that prioritise the needs and desires of the family or even community first over an individual's needs and desires. Any individual trying to assert their preferences over that of the community or family could face a lot of resistance, judgment, or verbal criticism.

Reasons People Don't Set Boundaries

Sneha and her family struggled with the lack of emotional privacy. The constant intrusion into personal matters by the extended family made it challenging for Sneha to assert boundaries despite living in a different city.

Jennifer was a young woman who was torn between pursuing her career aspirations and fulfilling familial expectations. Despite the stress and impact on her mental well-being, she prioritized family obligations over her own desires out of a sense of duty and eventually quit a job she loved.

Aman and his family, like many others, avoided conflicts at all costs. The pressure to maintain harmony suppressed individual voices, leading to unspoken tensions that erupted into huge conflicts more than once.

All these people struggled with boundary setting because of some cultural norms and conditioning that come with being a part of a collectivist culture. Other challenges that you can see popping up as you try to navigate boundary setting with family could include:

- Obligations or Expectations: In a collectivist culture, there is a huge expectation to fulfil familial obligations first before anything else. Many people do this even when it's tough for them. We're taught that it's normal to have these obligations and that we should fulfil them no matter what, even if it means putting our own lives on hold or facing challenges in our personal lives.

- Fear of disapproval: Many hesitate a lot to even think of holding a tiny boundary with family, let alone setting one, because of the fear of disapproval.

- Lack of privacy: We pride ourselves in being a part of a close-knit family. As amazing as that is, it makes boundary setting tricky because of limited personal space and privacy. A lack of emotional privacy can be challenging for families staying in different places too.

- Guilt: There is a strong sense of loyalty in everyone who comes from a collectivist culture. This innate feeling of loyalty can lead to a massive load of guilt when asserting personal boundaries, which can seem like a direct attack on the collectivist culture.

- Interdependence: In a collectivist culture, we take great pride in our interdependence where we rely on each other for emotional, mental, and financial support. While this is acceptable within healthy limits, it frequently becomes unhealthy and is sometimes exploited. When someone even tries to set personal boundaries, it might seem as if the entire balanced ecosystem of interdependence is threatened by just one boundary.

- Social pressure: One of the reasons why many people, even those who could set excellent boundaries, fail to do so with family is because of societal pressure. That doesn't spare anyone. There is immense pressure to conform to social and familial norms, which often results in people compromising their own priorities and preferences. It's easy to get the tag of being selfish or disrespectful if you choose to go against the tide, even for once.

- Conflict Avoidance: We do not like conflict, and we are not good at handling conflicts. Dodging conflicts comes so easily to us, and we fail to recognize that someone is probably compromising their own happiness in an attempt to avoid a conflict. There is pressure to not talk or do anything that causes disagreements or confrontations in the family. So, everyone walks on eggshells and never speaks up. I'm not advocating for conflicts; but, sometimes, avoiding them in the short term can be worse, as unresolved issues may escalate into unavoidable and more significant fights. It's a matter of choosing between smaller conflicts now or potentially larger ones later. What's your preference?

- Gossip: News travels at an unbelievable pace in a collectivist culture. You just need to share something with one person, and before you know it, everyone you know knows the news. If it's good news, it's fine, but news about someone trying to set boundaries can go down like wildfire. It could be exaggerated and blown out of proportion, and no one wants to deal with that drama. This is why many feel it's better to just not attempt to try such things and conform to what's acceptable.

There is also assumed responsibility on both genders. This is not unique to a collectivist culture since it is seen in individualistic culture as well. Women are assumed to take up the responsibility of managing work, household, kids, family, extended family, and dozens of other things. She doesn't try to set a boundary because she feels it's her responsibility to do it on her own. Or she's made to feel that way.

Men are expected to carry the financial burden of the family - both immediate and extended. This might mean helping out relatives in financial need, contributing to family events like weddings, or managing household finances, even if he is struggling to support himself. The thought of boundary setting doesn't come to him due to his sheer sense of duty.

While it was a hard fact a few years back, it has gotten a lot better now. We are getting more supportive and empathetic towards each other, but we still have a long way to go. Until then, unfortunately, many will hesitate to set family boundaries and continue to constantly give at the cost of their well-being.

Family, Self, Boundaries: Finding Balance

Setting boundaries within a collectivist culture requires a delicate balance between individual needs, cultural norms, and family traditions.

Apart from the above-stated reasons, many hesitate to set a boundary because they assume that other family members won't understand. I made this mistake until I tried to set a small boundary, and it was responded to with respect and support.

There is a very good chance the other family members will actually understand your reason for setting the boundary, but we just give up before we even try.

Boundary setting doesn't mean that you stop showing up for family just because you chose to show up for yourself too. Here's how you can involve them in the process and get them on board.

- Initiate an open conversation: An honest and respectful conversation can really go a long way. Explain why you need to set a certain boundary and emphasise that you are doing so to focus on your well-being, not to disrespect anyone. You can educate your family about the importance of personal boundaries, if necessary, and how they can actually improve and strengthen relationships.

- Involve elders. Seek the support of elders, who you think can smoothen the disruptions that may arise. Coming from an elder member or family authority figure can go a long way. If you have a grandparent who you feel will understand better than your parent, seek their support.

- Set clear expectations: As a general rule of thumb, you need to always set clear boundaries with anyone. But it becomes a bit more important with family. When there is a higher chance of things going south quickly because of the tiniest communication issues, it's better to always set crystal-clear boundaries. Use "I" statements liberally, as they will allow you to express your feelings without placing the blame on others.

- Offer alternatives or compromise: Here's another truth about setting boundaries within a family. You may not get complete autonomy to set your boundaries. But, you can offer compromises and alternatives that work and respect both you and the family. This is where you need to find the middle ground that works for both. Having too many rigid boundaries will probably not work well. Keep them flexible as much as you can.

- Start small: Another mistake you could make while setting boundaries with family is trying to set all boundaries at once or starting with a boundary that may be very hard for them to adapt to. Start small and make gradual changes. You will have better success.

Keep in mind that setting boundaries in collectivist cultures is a step-by-step journey. It might mean making compromises and keeping the communication lines open. The aim is to strike a balance that honours your personal needs while respecting the values of your culture and community.

Where & How to Set Boundaries in Family

Within a familial setting, you may need boundaries in different aspects. I'll try to cover a few common ones.

Boundaries in Parenting

Boundaries around parenting can be tricky with families. Parenting boundaries can be two-fold: a) boundaries that parents have with other family members with respect to their children, and b) boundaries that parents have for their kids.

Let's look at both and discuss them briefly.

Parenting with Boundaries – For Kids

Parents these days do not believe in 'spare the rod and spoil the child.' They do believe in tough love but also prioritise the emotional well-being of the kids. Every action is thought through with the intention that it doesn't hurt the child in the long run. Gentle parenting has shot up in popularity in the past few years, and for good reason. People are seeing great results of parenting consciously, gently, and intentionally.

Unfortunately, because it is termed 'gentle', parents often believe that it is only about displaying extreme gentleness and being permissive with little to no boundaries. Well, that is the exact opposite of what gentle parenting is all about.

A huge aspect of gentle parenting is about holding firm boundaries. As we've already seen, boundaries need to have consequences. When kids violate the boundaries, you need to have consequences, not punishments. The 'gentle' part is explaining the consequences gently and offering empathy when kids are upset about having to face the consequences.

You can start teaching about boundaries to your kids from a very young age. Within this, there are again two parts to teach - about how to respect the boundaries you've set and how they can convey their own boundaries to others.

Kids as young as one and a half years old can understand boundaries based on how you demonstrate it to them. Start with clearly explaining what boundaries actually mean, and what boundaries they need to adhere to.

Let them know clearly what the consequences are if they don't adhere to the boundary. Make sure it is not a punishment but a related consequence. The consequences could be something as simple as 'no screen time until homework is done' or 'you pay for the repair from your pocket money if you break it.'

But for all these to work, you have to follow the next points without fail.

- Be consistent: Kids need predictability. If you enforce boundaries inconsistently or shell out consequences once in a while, kids will never understand the concept of boundaries. They will not learn what you intend to teach them. Consistency is essential even for adults for boundary setting, but its importance shoots up with kids.

- Make sure boundaries and consequences are age-appropriate: You need to assign chores and activities and establish boundaries that are age-appropriate for your kids. Increase the responsibilities and boundaries as they grow.

- Encourage open communication: Kids love independence. Right from the moment they become mobile and are aware of their surroundings, they seek independence. Some boundaries will obviously be set for their safety, such as no jumping from high surfaces, no sticking fingers into electrical sockets, not playing with sharp things and the like. They may not like such boundaries, but explain to them that these hard boundaries are in place for their safety.

  Also, convey that while you need to stay firm on some hard boundaries, you can be flexible about others. This will help them explore independence with confidence and in a safe manner. Also, encourage them to have a dialogue with you if they desire more freedom and independence or if they feel restricted by the boundaries.

  When they know you are open to being flexible and giving alternate options, they will feel safer coming to you than trying potentially risky or dangerous things on their own.

- Sibling Relationships: If you have two or more kids, you must be privy to sibling conflicts. You must teach them how to resolve their conflicts respectfully and peacefully. Don't try to solve each and every conflict as they will not learn the art of conflict management, but set some ground rules or boundaries when it comes to conflicts.

Like respecting each other's personal space, borrowing with permission, respecting each other's belongings, no name-calling during a fight, and not hitting each other. Of course, step in if things get too intense.

As long as these boundaries are maintained during a fight, let them resolve conflicts on their own. Boundaries in sibling conflicts help them learn a very important skill – fighting in the right manner.

- Digital boundaries: You can also make boundaries around screen time. Discuss with them and come to an agreement on how much screen time your kids get. Encourage them to indulge in outdoor play, hobbies like painting or crafts, reading, etc.

  In a world where the internet is at their fingertips, you also need to educate your kids about online safety and set clear, red boundaries. This could include never sharing personal information with anyone over the internet, being cautious about the content they share or consume, clicking on suspicious links, or downloading unknown files.

  Encourage them to come to you immediately if anyone is forcing or compelling them to break these boundaries, and explicitly tell them just how dangerous crossing these boundaries could be, not just for them but for the entire family.

Teaching Kids to Convey Their Boundaries

It's a common saying - Kids see, kids do. Children may not always do what you say, but they will always do what they see you do. So, instead of just teaching them about setting boundaries, it's important that you practice what you preach by modelling this behaviour. Show them positive examples of boundary setting and healthy boundaries in your interactions with others.

Encourage kids to express their feelings honestly and openly.

Make sure they know you are willing to listen to them without judgment, that you don't want them to bottle up their emotions for your sake, and that you would rather have them speak freely.

Introduce the concept of consent at an early age and teach them how to react or respond when someone crosses their boundaries without consent. Encourage them to come to you or any trusted adult they know, without any fear or shame, when someone tries to cross their physical boundaries.

Equip older kids with effective ways to address boundary-related conflicts. It will help them navigate such conflicts with confidence, which they can carry into their adulthood as well.

Parenting Boundaries with Family

Parents are bombarded with parenting advice each day - from complete strangers to family members. Most of the advice comes with good intentions. However, parents need to discuss their parenting choices and decisions amongst themselves and figure out how to respond to the barrage of advice that comes their way every day.

You need to decide what works for you as a unit and what boundaries you need to set for the well-being of your kids and family as a whole. Then, you need to communicate the same to your family, friends, and others about why these boundaries are important for you and your partner.

I am a part of a few online communities made for mums, and not one day goes by when someone doesn't drop a message, crib, or rant saying that their parenting decisions are not respected by their family members. And through the conversations with others, they soon realise it's because they haven't set a boundary or are having a tough time maintaining the boundary they set.

These are some areas in which you can set boundaries, firm or flexible, with others when it comes to your parenting decisions.

- Food: Clearly communicate your preferences for your child's diet, including what you allow and disallow. For example, many parents nowadays follow practices like baby-led weaning, avoiding salt and sugar until the age of one, choosing to breastfeed until the child turns two, or refraining from introducing highly processed foods early on. While these are personal choices, there will likely be at least a few family members questioning these decisions, sharing how they did things differently. Expect some pushback not only from family but also from friends due to the non-traditional nature of these choices, but be clear about holding your food boundaries for your kids.

  Let them know clearly what the boundaries and consequences are. Explain why you made these choices if you feel the other person will understand. If you think they won't understand, don't bother or worry about explaining too much. You just stick to your guns and be firm about the boundaries.

- Around consent: Teach your kid about body boundaries, like saying no if they don't want to give a hug or kiss to a relative. Tell the elders that this is a firm boundary that you will refuse to budge on, and if the child says no, you will not try to convince them otherwise.

- Body images: Unfortunately, people often feel entitled to comment on a child's physical appearance. Some make hurtful remarks about a child's weight, while others make comments about the kid's habits and make inappropriate remarks about their complexion or personality. It's crucial to establish a firm boundary that clearly communicates your intolerance for such comments.

- Sharing information: Inform your family and friends that you do not want them to share information with your children that isn't age-appropriate without checking with you first. This could be pertaining to world news, something about the family, or even personal information that may not be age-appropriate for the child. Tell them you have set this boundary to protect your child's mental and emotional health.

These are some hard boundaries that you can set. Yes, it could be tricky boundaries to maintain these, but communication and sharing your reasons will help others understand your perspective and help you with your parenting instead of fighting with it.

In-Laws and Extended Family

The challenge of setting boundaries goes up a notch if you live in joint families and multigenerational houses.

I've witnessed both sides of the coin. I once met a lady who thrived in a multigenerational home with her in-laws and extended family. Among the many reasons for her contentment was the open communication about boundaries. Her in-laws didn't just respect them but actively supported her in maintaining them. She always spoke with joy about her in-law's family.

And then I know a few people who struggle to even get a word out. I had a colleague who would wake up at 4am, cook breakfast and lunch for every member of the house, head to work, check in on them from work, head back home, make snacks and dinner, clean the house, help the kid with her schoolwork, finish all the household chores, and get some meal prep done for the next day. On most days, she didn't get a chance to sleep before 12 at night. She did everything on her own for 7 members of the family, with no help from anyone.

The relentless cycle of early mornings and late nights left her thoroughly exhausted, leaving barely any time for rest. She tried communicating her boundaries once and was thoroughly shamed for it, after which she never tried. I have no idea if she ever got any help, but I'm sincerely hoping she's getting more than 4 hours of sleep each day, at the very least.

While it was her choice to take on the herculean task without trying to set boundaries, you don't have to do that if you're in the same boat as hers. Here's how you can make boundary setting a little more manageable in a joint family setup.

- If you live in a multigenerational family, make it a point for everyone to meet frequently to discuss household responsibilities and boundaries. You can call them family meetings or any other word that you deem appropriate, but the idea is to conduct it like a proper meeting. Encourage everyone to discuss their concerns, putting boundaries in place for everyone so that everyone feels comfortable and has their own space in such a large unit.

  Some members end up with most of the household responsibilities. You can use family meetings to ensure that all responsibilities are shared evenly without just a few feeling the entire pressure. When that happens, it may foster resentment, burnout, or exhaustion from managing the entire household of so many people.

- Encourage open dialogue across age groups, providing a platform for sharing experiences and expectations. Foster an environment where wisdom from older generations coexists with fresh insights from the younger ones. Promote mutual respect, recognizing that each generation brings valuable contributions to the family narrative.

- If the house is physically large enough, it would be a good idea to have some designated spots for individual family units. This will allow each family to have some independence and get time to spend amongst themselves. Having clear demarcations will prevent everyone from intruding on others' spaces or making someone uncomfortable. The designated spot allows each unit to do what they want as a family without feeling any judgment or pressure from others and get some time to bond.

Cultural Considerations

Nowadays, families are becoming culturally more diverse. Some family members could belong to a different culture, religion, state, or country. This could make boundary setting slightly tricky because what's normal in one culture may be considered inappropriate in other culture.

Suppose one spouse comes from a culture that emphasizes modesty in clothing, and the other is from a culture that doesn't have any such restrictions. Or picture a family where religious beliefs influence dietary choices. One partner may follow specific dietary restrictions based on their faith, while the other might not have such limitations. Negotiating these differences requires a sensitive approach to ensure that both individuals feel comfortable and respected in their choices.

With families getting diverse, it is important to engage in a respectful dialogue to understand each other's cultural norms. Talk about personal boundaries and help them understand your perspective of why you would need to set certain boundaries. Ask them about their boundaries and be genuinely interested to learn about their culture. This helps them open up and be reciprocal to your boundaries.

Encourage family members to share their cultural traditions, fostering a sense of inclusivity. Create an environment where everyone's customs are acknowledged and respected.

It's about recognizing the nuances of diverse cultural practices and working together to establish boundaries that honour and embrace the richness of both worlds.

Spousal Relationships

Though we have covered relationships in Chapter 4, let's take a quick glance again with respect to spousal relationships.

- Cultivate a unified approach to parenting: There are many styles of parenting, and it isn't necessary that both parents follow the same style. It's a good idea to have an open conversation about what values, expectations, and disciplinary methods you believe in and find a common ground that works for you both. You can have boundaries around some parenting aspects so that there is no miscommunication later. Being on the same page also helps in setting and maintaining consistent boundaries with other family members.

- Interacting with each other's families: Based on the relationship you share with your spouse's family, you can set boundaries that benefit your relationship. You can discuss the level of involvement you're comfortable with, the frequency of communication, and the expectations you have from their family. You need to strike a balance between familial bonds and boundaries to have a harmonious family environment.

- Co-parenting: Separated or divorced parents who co-parent their kids need to embrace a collaborative attitude. The only way to have a healthy co-parenting dynamic is through setting clear boundaries. You will have to make sure that there are consistent rules and expectations for children across both households.

- Blended families: The dynamics of a blended family can be challenging and complex initially. If possible, ask everyone what their boundaries are so that they feel acknowledged and seen. This will help you understand their expectations and challenges and make the transition a little easier for everyone. You need to set personal and family boundaries with the ex-partner and stepfamilies. It will help you develop a solid foundation for a close-knit, strong, blended family.

Financial Boundaries

This will be a tricky area to set boundaries in, but when you do, it can help mitigate conflicts around money. Unfortunately, family disputes due to money are a common thing in every household around the world.

Certain family members are expected to financially support others, but when they are taken advantage of, things get tricky. It's unfair to those who are willing to help but always end up getting burned in the process.

Talking openly about individual financial contributions and shared expenses would take out a lot of guesswork. If someone's feeling generous and wants to contribute beyond what is decided, that's perfectly fine. But expecting someone to contribute without considering the lender's financial scenario just because it's a 'family duty' can cause serious family rifts.

*** *** ***

One of my favourite examples of boundary setting in a family that portrays a lot of the points discussed above is from the show 'Modern Family'. Though the TV show deals with boundary issues comedically, there are some learning moments that we can all take away from.

In one episode, mom Claire insists on a structured approach to parenting, while dad Phil prefers a more laid-back style. Their conflicting parenting approaches to discipline highlighted the need for clear communication and compromise in setting parenting boundaries.

Jay and Gloria are a great example of a blended family with a mixed cultural background. There were many instances where the challenges and importance of setting boundaries in blended cultures and families were shown.

The three Dunphy siblings were very different from each other, and sibling conflicts were common in the household. While mom Claire wouldn't normally interfere in the fight, she made sure to remind them of boundaries while fighting - like no name calling, no hitting, etc.

I'm pretty sure you can find similar examples from your household, too, if you reflect a little.

*** *** ***

Navigating complex family dynamics with grace and clarity requires ongoing communication, empathy, and a commitment to shared values. By setting boundaries thoughtfully, families can create environments that foster understanding, respect, and lasting connections.

Setting boundaries in the areas discussed in this segment will help you get started, and you can tackle other areas depending on what your family uniquely faces.

One of the main reasons why family members struggle to set boundaries is their hesitation to say no or that they feel pressured to say yes to every single thing. It won't be resolved overnight, but this next activity will help you take the first step.

ACTIVITY 8: The 24-Hour Rule

This activity could probably be the easiest one to write about but the most difficult to implement of all the activities mentioned in the book. Probably because you need to do it as a family unit, and it may take a while for others to come on the same page as you.

Though it may be challenging to start this, when implemented, the 24-hour rule can be such a valuable tool for the entire family.

This activity is mainly to handle family requests and respond to them. This rule simply states that one should take 24 hours, at the very least, to consider and respond to requests made by any family member. This ensures that everyone thinks through their responses without feeling the pressure to say yes immediately and regret it later or feeling resentment for being forced into doing things because they were suddenly put on the spot.

Start with small discussions, and then eventually, you can tackle the topic of boundary setting. Convey your own personal boundaries and encourage others to convey theirs.

To get started, you can choose a simple, small request that you want the family to consider. It could be your request or someone else's. Request everyone to take 24 hours to consider the request. You can consider how the request aligns with your values - accept if it aligns, politely decline if it doesn't.

Communicate why you reached a particular choice or decision and answer any questions the family may have. Make sure you show respect, empathy, and kindness while communicating.

Once this activity is over, make sure you spend some time reflecting on how it worked for you. If you think it'll help, make and practice boundary scripts to be better prepared for unexpected or extreme reactions. Also, assess what didn't work for you and how you would tackle that the next time.

You can also encourage other family members to adopt this technique. As I said, it may take a while to be accepted by others, but you stick to it as much as possible. Eventually, others might come around or accept you doing it.

Conflict Resolution

One reality of boundary setting in families is that you will see conflicts at some point. While conflict is a possibility in every other area we discussed, it almost always is a guaranteed thing with families. That's just the nature of it and doesn't mean what you're doing is wrong or that their reaction is unwarranted.

Unlike other areas where you can distance yourself, like friends or work, boundary setting is slightly tricky in families, especially when you stay together.

Since we are so good at avoiding conflict and going out of the way to ensure that no situation leads to a conflict, a lot of us never really learned to deal with conflict in a healthy manner. I've seen a lot of people operating in the extremes - either doing everything possible to avoid a conflict or not talking to each other for years when conflicts do occur. Neither is healthy and is equally damaging to relationships in the long run.

When conflicts do arise, encourage family members to express their feelings instead of trying to bottle them up or bury them, which could lead to resentment. If you ask me, I would suggest you to choose conflicts over resentment any day.

One can be ugly in the short term, but resolving it will lead to a positive outcome, while the other may be good in the short term because you avoid it completely, but it can get really ugly in the long term.

Since conflicts are unavoidable in most cases, it's better to have some conflict management strategies up your sleeve. These could include active listening, finding common ground, using a mediator, brainstorming solutions together after everyone has calmed down, or apologizing and forgiving.

Don't try to resolve a conflict then and there if the emotions are really high. It's better to step away for a bit and give everyone a chance to cool down. Embrace moments of silence during the conflict instead of responding or reacting instantly. Silence will allow you to think before you respond and convey to the other person that you are interested in finding a solution that works for everyone instead of just fighting non-stop.

I came across an interesting conflict resolution technique a while back. I'll be honest; I've never tried, but do try it if you think it'll work for you. It's about doing a role reversal exercise to understand each other's perspective.

This exercise encourages you to switch places with each other and see the conflict from the other's point of view, which builds empathy. It can give you all a fair chance at arriving at a solution faster, but this technique probably won't work when everyone involved is feeling strong emotions and isn't willing to reverse roles at that moment.

Another great tip is to move to a neutral place when conflicts occur. I've heard of a couple who resolve their conflicts over a walk. They know they cannot raise their voice outside and will be forced to keep their calm. It has helped them resolve quite a few conflicts calmly.

Finally, humour is great at lightening the mood and breaking the tension. If it's appropriate, like in a small conflict that isn't too serious, you can try to add a little humour. The laughter can diffuse the tension and encourage everyone to approach the disagreement in a more positive manner.

Me vs Them

Striking a balance between family interdependence and individual autonomy can be an ongoing process. Foster open communication within the family, encouraging members to express their aspirations and goals. Creating shared family objectives is a wonderful way for everyone to feel aligned as a unit but also celebrate their individuality.

Whether you come from a nuclear family or a huge, joint one, focus on building a supportive atmosphere that recognizes and values both collective efforts and individual pursuits.

Boundary setting in a family can be mentally and emotionally challenging for some. Prioritize your mental well-being, encourage regular check-ins with everyone, and create a supportive environment for discussing mental health in the family. Focus on your self-care routines, whether it's taking time for hobbies, exercising, or practicing mindfulness.

The next exercise will help you tackle one of the biggest reasons why there are disappointments and conflicts in the family. When this one thing isn't managed properly, setting boundaries can get trickier and a tad more frustrating than usual.

ACTIVITY 9: Expectation-Setting Exercise

It is absolutely normal to have certain expectations within a family. They are a good thing, as we discussed in Chapter 4. But when expectations are misaligned or unrealistic, problems will arise in no time. It can be trickier to navigate that in the context of boundary setting.

This exercise will help you pre-empt that by setting the right expectations. You need to understand how the values and priorities of different family members align with yours and find a way to make it work so that everyone's happy.

Do this exercise before a conflict arises, when everyone is in a positive mood, rather than trying to do it in the middle of a conflict.

- Think about some family expectations that everyone seems to disagree about. It could be about something huge like the career you want to pursue or whom you would like to marry. Or you can start small and review expectations regarding attending family events that you were invited to but can't attend. Your decision will seem right to you and vice versa.

- Check each other's expectations and assess how comfortable you are with the expectations that others have for you. Also, look at which expectations you are willing to consider, even if they don't perfectly align with what you want.

- Next, consider the expectations that do not align with you at all and seem like it could lead to conflict in the future if you don't address it now.

- View these differences as an opportunity to talk to your family instead of seeing them as huge problems. Sit together and have an open conversation to understand each other's perspectives and reasons behind those expectations. Figure out together if there is any way to adjust or change those expectations and how everyone can be on the same page.

It may take a while to reach a place where everyone is fine with the set expectations, but it's always better to talk it out before the conflict can potentially arise.

This practice will encourage you to try to understand their values, perspectives, and boundaries, which, in turn, will encourage them to do the same for you.

Engage in empathy-building conversations with the important people in your life, including family members, friends, and colleagues. Try to understand their perspectives, values, and the boundaries they have. Encourage open, non-judgmental dialogue.

With families, it's just a matter of holding your ground politely and sticking to it. It may take a while, but you'll find a way to make it work eventually.

We have covered four major areas of life where you should set boundaries. Now, just one major area is left.

*** *** ***

In a Nutshell

> Balancing individual requirements with cultural norms and family values is crucial when establishing family boundaries.
> Don't assume others won't understand your need for boundaries.
> Focus on one aspect initially to make the process smoother.
> Encourage family participation in suggested boundary activities to promote unity, ensuring greater success in setting and maintaining boundaries.
> Set the right expectations to make the process smoother.

Boundaries in Social Life

"Daring to set boundaries is about having the courage to love ourselves even when we risk disappointing others."

- Brené Brown

7

Think about your top 5 favourite memories.

Is at least one of them in a social setting, like with friends or cousins? It would be a reasonable assumption that a good chunk of our favourite memories would be with friends or some social circle.

Since we have covered social scenarios involving your partner, family, and colleagues in the previous chapters, let's focus specifically on social circles involving friends in this chapter.

Just like in romantic relationships, setting boundaries in social life doesn't even cross our minds. Why would it when hanging out with friends is all laughter, jokes, fun, and then some more laughter?

I'm here to gently nudge you and say, "You need to set boundaries with friends!"

Social commitments are an integral part of our lives. However, not all social engagements are created equal. Some align with our values, priorities, and well-being and bring us absolute joy, while others may drain our time and energy.

This chapter is about understanding the importance of evaluating and prioritizing these commitments to ensure that they align with who you are and what you stand for.

The Landscape Analogy

Picture your social life as a vast landscape that you have to navigate daily. Just as an actual landscape has peaks and valleys, your social life will have peaks and valleys, too.

Peaks refers to the social commitments and moments that make you feel alive. These are the commitments that nourish your soul, feel like a warm hug, bring you great joy, and, most importantly, align with your priorities and values.

But not all social commitments are the same. Some feel really draining, you dread attending them, and they always make you question why you accepted the invitation in the first place. These commitments go against your priorities and values and feel very unfulfilling. These are the valleys or dips in your social life landscape. Attending these 'valley' events can leave you feeling burnt out and stretched thin if they become too frequent.

It really is okay to say no to some social commitments if you don't feel like going. Just like in romantic relationships, work, and family life, it is a good idea to evaluate your values and priorities when it comes to social commitments.

Identifying Social Peaks and Valleys Using Priorities

Your priorities will once again be your cornerstone in identifying what is important to you, what isn't, and where to set the boundaries.

If it's family time, then it's a no-brainer that any social commitment connected to family will take precedence over any other social event.

If you're at a phase where friendships are the biggest priority, then plans with friends will trump everything else.

The next activity will help you get clarity on that.

ACTIVITY 10: Social Commitment Audit

Let's identify the peaks and valleys of your social life.

- Create a list of all the upcoming and current social commitments that you have to attend. Include recurring events like weekly outings or occasional get-togethers.

- Evaluate how each commitment aligns with your current priorities.

- Next, rank or categorise all these social commitments based on their alignment with your priorities.

- Commitments aligning with your priorities are your peaks, and those that don't are the valleys.

You can either reduce the 'valley' commitments or draw some boundaries around them and explore or prioritise the 'peak' commitments. Doing this will make your social life more balanced, leaving you feeling fulfilled and joyous.

You probably noticed how your priorities keep shifting, right? So, it's essential to adjust your boundaries accordingly. During college or pre-marriage days, socializing with friends might be a norm, but when family and kids enter the scene, commitments tend to change. Don't stress about it. After that season of life, hanging out with friends will likely become a top priority again.

Of course, there's absolutely no rule that you should not attend the 'valley' events at all. Sometimes, it is unavoidable, and you have to attend them. As with everything, you'll have to use your judgement and decide which ones can be skipped and which ones make the cut. That's just the reality of life. Sometimes, you have to attend valley events even if they don't align with your priorities. The one way you can manage your energy on such occasions is to have a flexible boundary, like leaving early.

Limit such occasions, but don't be rigid. After all, you need social interactions and relationships in your life, and it cannot always be all about you.

The one time it has to be about you is when peer pressure is involved.

Navigating Peer Pressure

We all have been there. We just do not feel like going to that lunch, movie, or a last-minute get-together for whatever reason, but we still put on our best and show up. We may not enjoy it, but dare we show it. We plaster that smile and pretend the evening away that we are having the best time of our lives.

This is us succumbing to peer pressure.

We mostly associate the word' peer pressure' with school- and college-going kids. It's probably because we think it's easier to give in to peer pressure at that age and believe we don't fall for it as we grow older.

Well, turns out we don't outgrow it. No matter what age you are, you will feel the psychological and emotional impact of peer pressure. That's the unfortunate truth that probably a lot of us want to deny.

The Impact of Peer Pressure

Many of us succumb to peer pressure or go ahead with honouring social commitments even when we don't want to. It could be because of one or more of the following reasons:

- Fear of Isolation – Nobody wants to feel isolated, especially when you have a huge set of friends.

- Fear of Confrontation: Many just don't like the conflicts or confrontations that may arise due to setting boundaries or saying no, so they just go along with something even when they don't want to.

- Desire to Fit in: Conformity can be a result of wanting to be a part of a social group, especially if you can be perceived as the 'cool kid's group' and tags that people may like.

- Desire for Acceptance: It's an innate human desire to feel accepted and belong to a social group. There is nothing wrong with that until peer pressure causes someone to go to extreme lengths to be accepted, like a non-smoker having to smoke just because he has to fit in.

- Fear of Letting Others Down: Another common reason why people give in to peer pressure is that they don't want to disappoint their friends. They prioritise the harmony of the group over their own preferences, priorities, and values.

- Lack of Alternatives: If someone has fewer friends, they will tend to do everything the group asks them to do because they have nowhere else to go.

- Unawareness of Personal Boundaries: This is the most common one. When you are unaware that there is a concept called boundaries or that you can have boundaries with friends, you may just follow what the group wants without questioning anything.

Peer pressure may sound like an ugly word, but let's call a spade a spade.

Here's a common instance that happens in every single group. This instance is a perfect example where one can feel peer pressure due to a lack of boundaries. This happens around a meal table with friends, all having different food-eating choices. There will be someone telling the others whose food choices are different to try out their food. It could be said as a joke, with genuine intentions, or forcefully.

It can play out in a few ways.

Firstly, there are those with firm boundaries around their food.

They can confidently say no without succumbing to pressure.

Then, there are individuals who feel strongly about their eating choices but struggle to establish boundaries or are uneasy about setting them. This group may experience discomfort and pressure, and I've even witnessed a few of them break down due to the constant jibes and remarks about their preferences. It can be tough for them to navigate social situations where their food choices are scrutinized or belittled.

And finally, there are some folks who are open to experimenting. They willingly give new dishes a shot and might even enjoy the experience.

How you handle and respond to their decisions is crucial. If you respect their 'no' and move on, that's perfectly fine—it should be that way. However, if you force them to eat against their will, that's peer pressure.

In a supportive and considerate friend circle, there's no pushing or pressurising. Unfortunately, not everyone's social circle is as understanding. In some cases, peer pressure disguises itself as friendly banter or fun, coercing you time and again.

Forms of Coercion

We tend to think of 'peer pressure' as something only school kids deal with because we usually connect it with doing risky or undesirable things, like bullying, ragging, or experimenting with substances.

Things like teasing, pulling each other's legs, jokes, and sarcasm are all common in a friend's circle. But, it qualifies as fun only when everyone is on the same page and genuinely enjoy these light-hearted moments.

It's important to understand if the other person is having fun or feeling pressurised. Peer pressure has a factor of coercion to it. If someone repeatedly forces and pressurises you to do something that you just don't want to do despite you clearly communicating it, that's peer pressure and coercion, not friendly teasing.

So, how do we identify coercion?

- Direct pressure: Sometimes, there's no sugar-coating. This involves explicit demands or persuasion from friends to engage in specific actions.

- Indirect pressure: This is observed when peers don't want to tell you directly but will go out of their way to make you feel left out if you don't conform to what they want, like excluding you from social gatherings or plans.

- Verbal manipulation: This happens when people use verbal approaches like guilt-tripping or false flattery to make you comply. If someone repeatedly says things like "But you're so good at it, that's why we need you," or "If you consider me to be your friend, you'll do it." Real friends wouldn't put that kind of pressure on you, and if they really needed your help with something, they would directly say that instead of spinning it and making you do the work for them.

- Teasing: This isn't the fun teasing that I'm talking about, but a more serious one. It happens when peers taunt or tease someone with malicious intent. This is usually observed when there is risky behaviour at play. It may sound like "You're such a scaredy cat, we know you can't handle something like this!" People may find themselves doing things they don't want to do, only to avoid this kind of teasing.

- Social comparison: When they go to the lengths of comparing you with others in the group specifically to make you feel less about yourself.

- Social media pressure: We've seen tons of cases where people took on reckless social media challenges, and sadly, some even paid the price with their life — all thanks to social media peer pressure. It's like people feel this pressure to join the 'cool' club and do risky online challenges like eating Tide Pods, even if the others involved are total strangers they've never met.

Most don't encounter these issues in their group, but unfortunately, some aren't as fortunate. People who don't have good friends may feel tremendous mental and emotional distress. They may start sacrificing their own values, engage in risk-taking behaviour, ignore personal boundaries, and feel low self-esteem.

If you feel you fall into this category, you need to work on the techniques we'll discuss next. Even if you have the greatest friends, go through this section because you can help someone in a tricky social situation or apply these techniques for boundary setting in other areas of your life that need work.

Mastering Assertive Refusal

These techniques, exactly like the name suggests, are about assertively refusing to do something. Assertively saying "no" is a crucial aspect of setting boundaries.

As easy as it is to understand this, it can be difficult to implement it, especially with close friends whom you have known for years. But just like any other skill, you can learn, develop, or improve it.

If you're caught up in a million 'what will they think' scenarios running through your mind, remember, they're most likely just in your head. We often tend to overthink and blow things out of proportion, assuming our friends won't understand. In reality, the chances are high that they will.

If they don't, it could be time to rethink your social circle. I'm being a bit straightforward here, but sometimes, a reality check nudges us to make the necessary changes.

Just remember, saying no assertively is like having your own back while still respecting others. It's a skill that grows over time, letting you navigate social life with confidence and keep your well-being in check.

Assertive Communication Techniques

I am listing 5 techniques that will help you set boundaries effectively. When applied correctly, these techniques work wonders.

Note that while I'll be speaking only in the context of social circles, you can apply these techniques to set boundaries in every area of life.

1. "I" Statements

We've already covered this in chapter 4, but let's take a quick look again just because of how powerful this technique is.

"I" statements work well because you put the spotlight on your feelings and emotions rather than blaming the other person. They help you assert your boundaries confidently while being respectful to others.

How to use it:

Situation	'I' Statement
Invitations to events	You: "I appreciate the invitation, but I have other commitments and priorities and won't be able to make it."
Constant unannounced visits	You: "I value our friendship, but I need some advance notice when you plan to visit. It helps me prepare and ensures I can give you my full attention."

Sharing personal information	You: "I want you to know that I value your friendship, but there are certain things I prefer to keep private. It's not about you; it's about my own comfort. I hope you understand."
Borrowing personal items	You: "I'm happy to help, but I've realized that I'm uncomfortable lending out personal items, especially jewellery. I'm happy to lend anything else, but not this. It's not personal; it's just how I feel about my belongings."

2. Broken Record Technique

The core idea of this communication technique is to calmly yet repeatedly assert your boundaries without getting pulled into an argument.

It may seem annoying to others, but it conveys that you have an unwavering stance. It shows that you cannot be easily influenced or pressured to do something that goes against your choices. This works great in situations when someone is trying to pressurise you through persistence.

I immediately thought of my friend Azim when I learned about the broken record technique. After a health scare, he kicked off his fitness journey and switched into full health-conscious mode. Committed to embracing a healthier lifestyle, he diligently followed the dietary recommendations from both his fitness trainer and doctor.

Whenever he went out with friends, everyone would usually order something that wasn't a part of his diet plan. So, he often chose to order separately for himself. This caused his friends to tease him or force him to eat whatever they ordered instead of ordering separately for himself.

When his friends pulled his leg about trying to be healthy, he would just laugh it off and repeat he wanted to stick to his food choices and preferences. At some point, his friends realised he wouldn't budge and they stopped bothering him altogether. What's more, some even got inspired by him and got into fitness!

It all started because he chose to follow the broken record technique, and he wasn't even aware of it.

How to use it:

Situation	Broken Record Response
Being persuaded to attend events you don't want to go to or can't attend	Them: "Come to the concert with us!" You: "I appreciate the invitation, but I'll pass on this one. Have fun without me!" Use the same response each time they bring it up.
Frequent requests for favours	Them: "Can you do me a favour this weekend?" You: "I wish I could, but I've got other commitments. I'm sorry." Reiterate if they keep asking without getting into an argument.

Receiving unwanted criticism or advice	Them: "You should really change your job."
	You: "I hear you and appreciate your concern, but I'm satisfied with my career. Let's talk about something else."
	Repeat as necessary, ensuring it doesn't lead to conflict.
Pressure to share personal information	Them: "Why don't you tell us your secret?"
	You: "I prefer to keep certain things private. Thanks for understanding."
	Repeat it in a calm manner without getting aggressive if they keep asking you the same question.

The trick here is to repeat the same answer over and over again without justifying it too much.

3. Fogging

All of us have definitely used this technique. We just didn't know that it was called fogging.

In this technique, you acknowledge the validity of someone's statement without becoming defensive or explicitly agreeing with it.

This tactic works well to avoid conflicts that may go south. Fogging shows that you are open to listening to what others have to say about your choice, but you won't compromise on your values or boundaries.

The key is not to get defensive or rude.

How to use it:

Situation	Fogging Response
Negative comments on your personal choices	Them: "You're making a bad decision." You: "I appreciate your perspective, and I understand what you're saying, but I'm comfortable with my choice." Maintain a calm demeanour.
Pressure to attend an event you don't want to or can't attend	Them: "You must come to the party!" You: "Thanks for inviting me and I know it'll be a lot of fun. I understand it's important to you, but I'm sorry I won't be able to make it this time." Keep it neutral.

Unwanted critique of your lifestyle	Them: "You should really change your diet." You: "I understand you're concerned, but I've got a plan that works for me. Let's agree to disagree." Stay diplomatic.
Pressure to share your personal life	Them: "Why are you so secretive?" You: "I understand you're curious, but I prefer to maintain some privacy. It's just my preference." Keep it non-confrontational.

4. Non-Verbal Assertiveness

Not everything that you need to communicate has to be verbal. You can show assertiveness through non-verbal actions like raising your hand or moving away.

Non-verbal assertiveness sends a strong message to the other person. If they pick up on it, they'll respect your boundary without you needing to vocalize it. If the non-verbal cues aren't clear to them, you can then explicitly state your boundary.

Ria was comfortable hugging her friends, but she didn't like hugging someone she just met, irrespective of gender. When she went to a friend's birthday party, she hugged all her friends, but when she was introduced to a friend's friend, she moved back a little to show that she wasn't comfortable hugging. The other girl, who was a big hugger, immediately understood the gesture and gave Ria a handshake instead.

There were no words exchanged to communicate the boundary. Just a non-verbal cue, and it worked like a charm.

How to use it:

Situation	Non-Verbal Response
Someone invades your personal space	Stepping back or creating physical distance, raising a hand to signal "stop," or using body language to convey discomfort.
A colleague consistently borrows your belongings without asking	Clearly labelling and organizing your personal space, using non-verbal cues, like a head shake or adjusting your belongings to convey a sense of personal boundaries.
Someone consistently interrupts you during a conversation	Gently raising a finger to signal for a moment of uninterrupted speaking, maintaining eye contact to convey the desire for respectful communication.

5. Reflective Listening

This communication tactic works well in situations where you find yourself caught off-guard and don't know how to respond immediately. It gives you some time to think and come up with an answer.

Reflective listening allows you to convey that you've comprehended the other person's question or statement by either rephrasing or repeating what they said or asking clarifying questions. This not only assures them that you've truly understood their perspective but also provides you with a moment to gather your thoughts and respond assertively.

It may take a while to get good at this because you have to think on the spot, but it's a great tactic to make others feel genuinely heard and ensure that your own thoughts are acknowledged in the process.

How to use it:

Situation	Reflective Listening Response
A friend questions your decision, catching you off-guard.	You: "It sounds like you're curious about why I made that choice. Let me make sure I understand your concern before I respond. Can you clarify what you're questioning specifically?"
Someone confronts you about a personal matter without warning.	You: "I wasn't expecting to discuss this right now. Let me make sure I understand your perspective. Can you share more about what's on your mind before I respond?"

A friend unexpectedly shares a personal detail about you in a group setting.	You: "I wasn't prepared for that information to be shared. To make sure I understand the intent, can you help me understand why you felt it was necessary to bring that up in this context?"

These techniques will help you convey your boundaries confidently.

But to up your assertiveness game and take your confidence to the next level, you will need boundary scripts.

ACTIVITY 11: Make Assertive Refusal Boundary Scripts

Develop boundary scripts using the 5 assertive communication techniques we discussed. Try to focus on instances that you occasionally face or may anticipate when you set a boundary with your friends.

These scripts will give you time to prepare and rehearse so that when the time comes to actually say those things, you say it with so much confidence that people don't question your assertiveness. It ensures that you're never caught off-guard.

Some examples of boundary scripts to get you started:

1. "I appreciate the invitation, but I won't be able to come. I know I agreed earlier, but I can't make it because of some personal situation. I hope you have a fantastic time, though."

2. "I value your input, but I'm comfortable with my choice.

Let's respect each other's decisions."

3. "I value our relationship, but I also need to maintain balance in my life. Let's find a middle ground."

4. "I understand your need, but I won't be able to help with this. I can connect you with someone who can help you if you want."

Make sure you maintain a firm yet polite tone while being assertive and clear.

Repeating Activity: Role-Playing Assertive Responses

It goes without saying that all these tactics and scripts need practice. You just cannot hope to remember them and craft a response on the spot.

Bring out your boundary buddies and practice these techniques and scripts through role-playing.

Practice navigating common social situations that you often find yourself in, like declining a social event, sticking to your preferences or choices of food, not smoking or drinking, getting home early, etc.

Practice in a safe environment where you don't feel any pressure, as this will help in building your confidence.

Some other things that you can consider when you find yourself in a tricky social situation that can violate your boundaries are:

- Using humour: Humour is a great way to diffuse a tense situation, especially amongst friends.

- Walk away: If you feel the pressure is getting too much, it's always better to walk away, even if it's for a few minutes. Head back in when things are calmer and discuss, or you can always leave if it's too intense.

- Offer alternatives: If you can find any alternate solution, put it forward. This shows that you are willing to compromise a little without violating personal boundaries.

- Say 'Maybe': If you're in a spot where saying a straight-up 'no' might bring on some negativity, or you're not quite sure how to respond just yet, go with a 'maybe'. It gives you the time to think things over without feeling rushed or pressured.

  But here's the thing—don't make 'maybe' your default answer for everything because it might sneakily transform into a 'yes' more often than you'd like. Set a monthly quota for your 'maybes' and stick to it.

  On the other hand, if you're always in the 'maybe' zone, people might stop counting on you. They could think you're all talk and no action, and that's not what you want. You might end up missing out on stuff you'd actually be into.

Finally, trust your gut. If something doesn't feel right, it's a sign that your boundaries are being challenged. Learn to listen to your instincts.

You have now looked into how to set boundaries at work, in relationships, in family, in social circles, and in your own self. But we have a much bigger beast to tame. I'm pretty sure you are familiar with it and probably wondering how to tackle this part of boundary setting – feeling guilt, fear, hesitation, anxiety, and everything negative that probably comes as an unwanted bonus of boundary setting!

*** *** ***

In a Nutshell

- > Not all social commitments are equal. Identify which give you joy and prioritise and set boundaries around the ones that don't

> Be aware of peer pressure and different forms of coercion.
> Work on assertive communication techniques to set boundaries with more confidence.
> Practice boundary-setting through role-playing scenarios with boundary buddies.

142

143

Managing Negative Emotions and Feelings

"When you say 'yes' to others, make sure you are not saying 'no' to yourself."

- Paulo Coelho

SAY YES TO YOU

8

How do you feel when you set a boundary? Which emotion often comes up? How do others respond?

In the world of boundary setting, emotions can run high. Either you may feel something intense or the person with whom you're setting the boundary may respond negatively.

In order to manage them, you first need to be aware of which emotions surface for you.

In the earlier chapters, I mentioned about noticing body sensations or feelings to spot any boundary issues. I highlighted that your body would show clear signs. I used to do this often to because it worked for me, and then I found William James' Theory of Emotions.

William James, a prominent American psychologist and philosopher, introduced the James-Lange theory of emotions. According to this idea, our body reacts physically before we feel emotions. For instance, if we see a snake, our hearts might race before we consciously feel fear. While James' theory laid the foundation for understanding the link between bodily responses and emotions, it has been refined over time.

This is why your body responds to anything unpleasant, like a boundary violation, even before your brain fully registers it.

Back in 1890, he proposed that humans have four basic emotions – love, fear, grief, and rage. A hundred years later, in the 1990s, Paul Ekman (renowned American psychologist and a pioneer in the study of emotions and facial expressions) added more emotions to the list. It included positive and negative emotions - contempt, embarrassment, amusement, guilt, relief, satisfaction, and shame, to name a few, all of which could be linked to facial expressions.

In 1996, Richard Lazarus and Bernice Lazarus, both prominent figures in the field of psychology, expanded the list to 15 emotions. They included gratitude, envy, hope, jealousy, and fright.

Thanks to researchers at the University of California, Berkeley, we now know that there are 27 categories of emotions - admiration, adoration, aesthetic appreciation, amusement, anger, anxiety, awe, awkwardness, boredom, calmness, confusion, craving, disgust, empathic pain, entrancement, excitement, fear, horror, interest, joy, nostalgia, relief, romance, sadness, satisfaction, sexual desire, and surprise.

How many of these do you feel when you have to set boundaries? When it comes to setting boundaries, you might experience a single emotion or a combination of feelings before, during, or after the process. At the same time, the person on the other end can also feel a bunch of these emotions based on how easily they accept your boundaries.

Recognizing and Tackling 'Boundary Emotions'

It'll be pretty reasonable to say that most of the emotions felt by every party involved would be negative, at least in the beginning.

Managing these negative emotions can be quite tricky. What makes it even more challenging is that these emotions don't magically disappear after the first time you set boundaries. You may encounter these feelings every time you need to establish boundaries, regardless of your skill in the task.

The first few tries might be tough, but over time, you'll get the hang of it. They won't completely go away, but dealing with them will become much easier.

Once you are aware of which emotions seem to bubble up, it'll be easier for you to manage them.

So, which one of these do you feel the most when it comes to boundary setting?

Guilt

Guilt is the most common feeling when setting boundaries. It's especially at a peak when you have to say 'no' to people close to you. People who have a very strong sense of duty will feel guilt day in and day out, which is exactly why they stop prioritising themselves. In terms of a bodily response, guilt feels like a heaviness in the chest.

Guilt Management Strategies

- Reframe your perspective: Recognise that boundaries are an act of self-care (discussed in detail in Chapter 3) and not selfishness. This will make it easier to manage guilt because it will reaffirm your belief that saying 'no' isn't a bad thing.

- Self-Compassion Practices: You can practice mindfulness or spend some time on self-reflection to gain a deeper understanding of your thoughts and emotions, promoting personal growth and emotional well-being.

Dipika grappled with the infamous mom guilt every time she contemplated dedicating just an hour for herself for self-care. Even her family thought that an hour away from the toddler was a big ask. The weight of the guilt prevented her from setting a firm boundary.

However, a shift in perspective occurred when she recognized that her well-being directly impacted her ability to be a joyful and engaged mother. Exhaustion and frustration were taking a toll on her parenting, making it feel like a forced duty rather than a joy.

She gathered some courage and set a non-negotiable boundary. She sat her family down and sought their support, explaining the need for an hour of personal time. They finally understood her perspective and came together to give her some 'me time'. This not only provided Dipika the space she needed but also reignited her enjoyment of motherhood.

Although the guilt lingered, managing it for just an hour made the rest of the day more manageable without the weight of anger or frustration.

Fear of Conflict

Nobody likes conflicts, but some are good at managing or resolving them, while others shudder even at the thought of a possible conflict. The latter group of people are exactly those who consciously avoid setting boundaries just because of the fear of conflict.

It's not just being scared of disagreements; they also worry about what others might think. This fear is deeply rooted in how we're brought up, especially through cultural conditioning, which prioritizes keeping things calm, even if it means ignoring what one personally needs.

Strategies to Manage Fear of Conflict

- Shift Mindset: View conflicts as opportunities for growth and understanding rather than threats. Embrace the idea that healthy conflicts can lead to stronger, more authentic relationships.

- Gradual Exposure: If you feel you aren't ready to handle huge conflicts just yet, gradually expose yourself to small conflicts. You can do this by trying to set boundaries with people you know wouldn't react too negatively, and even if there is a small argument, it'll be easy to settle with them.

It could be with your partner or a close friend. Managing small disagreements will eventually build your resilience and confidence.

- Assertiveness Training: Learn and practice assertive communication skills we discussed in the previous chapter. This will help you express your needs confidently and navigate conflicts constructively

Resentment

This emotion sneaks up quietly as it builds up over time and has the power to unquestionably damage relationships. Resentment occurs when you feel neglected, don't get any appreciation or acknowledgment when you do things for others, or when others repeatedly take advantage of you, like knowingly crossing your boundaries because they believe you will understand.

If not managed, the person holding onto the resentment will burst at some point, after which all hell breaks loose.

Resentment Management Strategies

- Set Clear and Realistic Expectations: One of the main reasons why resentment starts brewing in any relationship is due to misaligned or unrealistic expectations. Communicate your expectations and boundaries clearly, and have realistic expectations to avoid disappointment.

  If you know someone may struggle with your boundaries, don't naively hope they will be fine and then get upset when they aren't. In such cases, anticipate some disappointment and discuss how to get on the same page instead of fostering resentment thinking they didn't support you immediately.

- Address Concerns Immediately: As soon as some issues arise, address them immediately without giving them any chance to marinate over time into something ugly. Even if timely communication results in conflicts, it's fine because handling conflicts is more manageable than built-up resentment.

- Open Communication: To keep things positive and avoid any lingering resentment, foster an environment of open communication. Share your limits, so everyone knows what works for you and what doesn't. It helps set clear boundaries and lets others understand your needs.

Sonia and Yash were a young working couple. Yash was dedicated to his demanding IT job, often working long hours to meet tight deadlines. Sonia, a freelancer, efficiently managed her work alongside household responsibilities.

Over time, Sonia began to feel neglected as Yash, caught up in work stress, unintentionally overlooked her needs and efforts. Assuming Sonia's understanding nature, Yash frequently crossed boundaries, such as scheduling work calls during their quality time.

Resentment quietly simmered within Sonia. Small gestures that once brought joy now caused emotional distress. Realizing that suppressing her frustration would only intensify the resentment, Sonia decided to address the concerns immediately. This allowed both of them to express their needs and boundaries calmly, preventing the build-up of resentment.

Sonia's swift action not only resolved the immediate issues but also strengthened their relationship, preventing further damage due to resentment.

Self-Doubt

You have self-doubt when you don't feel confident about setting boundaries or question their effectiveness. A nagging voice in your head will let you know if you are feeling this emotion.

It will make you question the need of your desire and whether you even deserve it or not. If you allow it, self-doubt will consume you, and you will never get through the process of boundary setting.

Or, you might not succeed even if you give it a shot because you won't put in the effort to keep the boundaries.

Strategies to Handle Self-Doubt

- Cultivate Self-Awareness: You already spent a good amount of time doing this through the different activities discussed in the book. Reflect on values, needs, and priorities to reinforce the legitimacy of your boundaries. Lean on your values and priorities list as and when you feel any self-doubt.

- Challenge Negative Self-Talk: Notice the little voice in your head and challenge it with positive affirmations. Remind yourself that your voice is just a result of others' opinions and thoughts and that you are bigger than your doubt.

- Seek Support: Sometimes, it gets easier to handle self-doubt when you get external validation. Reach out to trusted friends and loved ones for validation and support. Seek their help to overcome self-doubt.

Ananya, a budding stylist and content creator from a small town, dreamed of working alongside big names in the media industry. She often questioned the worth of her passion for fashion and doubted whether she deserved recognition. Without her family's support, she frequently dismissed her creative pursuits, contemplating a conventional career instead. This self-doubt hindered her from approaching clients and showcasing her work.

Despite the challenges, Ananya's passion was unrelenting. She decided to challenge her negative self-talk, making her love for fashion a significant part of her identity. Seeking support from friends who admired her courage and dreams, Ananya gradually learned to silence her self-doubt. Now thriving as a stylist in her dream city of Mumbai, Ananya's journey towards achieving her dreams has accelerated. While she is yet to work with the clientele she aspires to, overcoming self-doubt has propelled her forward on her chosen path.

Awkwardness

Setting boundaries is uncomfortable, especially when you are new to the game and don't really know its 'rules'. It can be awkward and uneasy to challenge the norm and try to do something that can be new for many.

Awkwardness or discomfort mainly stems from the fear of what others will think or feel about boundaries.

Strategies to Tackle Awkwardness

- Embrace It: This can seem very counterproductive, but it works. Accept that discomfort is a natural part of change and is a temporary feeling that accompanies personal growth.

- Develop Boundary Scripts: You have already done this activity for multiple areas where you need to set a boundary. The process of scripting makes the process feel more structured and less awkward.

- Practice in Low-Stakes Environment: Practicing in a safe and low-stakes environment will help you build confidence before being exposed to more challenging scenarios. When you do it many times, your responses become automatic. So, when a tough situation comes up, your brain handles it easily because you've practiced enough, and it feels normal instead of awkward.

Anger

Handling anger when people ignore or don't understand your boundaries is a common challenge. It stems from the frustration of feeling misunderstood or unacknowledged. To manage this anger, you need good communication skills to explain your point of view and help others understand.

Strategies to Address Anger in Misunderstanding

- Clarify Your Intentions: Clearly articulate why you need to set a specific boundary. Providing context and explaining the positive impact it has on your well-being can help others understand better.

- Educate About Boundaries: In some cases, individuals may not grasp the concept of personal boundaries. Take the opportunity to educate them on the importance of boundaries for mental and emotional health.

- Seek Common Ground: Find areas where your need for boundaries aligns with values or goals you share with the other person. Emphasize that setting boundaries is not about distancing but about creating a healthier, more respectful connection.

Effectively dealing with anger when there's a lack of understanding is crucial for creating a more harmonious and supportive environment that respects personal boundaries. Using these strategies can help achieve this goal.

We've covered some of the most commonly felt emotions while setting boundaries. The reality is everyone feels these emotions. You cannot skip or overlook this aspect of boundary setting. But you can definitely learn to tame them.

How quickly you learn to manage these emotions depends on your comfort level, adaptability skills, and your personality. Some can achieve it in days, and some can take months. But if you are consistent, you will get to a point where you can control these emotions instead of them controlling you.

The Art of Saying 'No'

Right at the beginning of the book, we saw that setting boundaries isn't just saying 'no' all the time. But it is a huge part of it, and you probably aren't good at it, or else you wouldn't have picked up this book.

If the thought of saying no causes beads of sweat on your forehead, gets your hands clammy, drives a million thoughts through your mind, and pounds your heart almost out of your chest in a matter of seconds, you aren't alone. This is precisely why so many people refrain from setting boundaries in the first place.

So, what do you do? I'm guessing that you decide to do it next time, and then the next, until the right moment never quite arrives. Either you keep postponing setting boundaries or stumble when attempting to do so, letting all the emotions tied to boundary setting control you indefinitely.

Alright, that was probably a little dramatic, but you know what I'm talking about. Consistency is key to setting and maintaining healthy boundaries, and you have to keep at it relentlessly to master boundary setting.

But there's one huge factor, bigger than even consistency, courage, or determination, that will define how successful you'll be in boundary setting. That factor is an 'identity shift'.

You absolutely have to embrace the identity of someone who is comfortable saying no. If you believe to your core that you can never be that person, you will always struggle to put yourself first. If you are unwilling to make that shift, then probably none of these tools and strategies will work for you in the long term.

You can learn how to implement it, and it may work for a while. However, if you consistently believe that you can't say no, it won't be long before you revert to your old identity, starting the cycle all over again. Embracing the identity of someone who loves saying yes to themselves and is comfortable saying no when necessary makes it much easier to apply all the discussed tools, techniques, and strategies.

If you're committed to changing the labels you give yourself and adopt the identity of someone who loves setting boundaries, is willing to try out all the techniques, and ready to overcome the fear or guilt of saying no, I'm here to make the 'saying no' part a little easier for you in the next section.

Different Ways to Say No

The easiest way to 'say no' is to embrace the 2-year-old in you! Confused?

Let's go back a few decades to when you were just a child. Ask your parents how easily you said no, and that too with unparalleled confidence. It just shows that we always knew how to say no. Observe any toddler, and you'll be impressed with the confidence with which they'll say no to things.

Somewhere down the road, what used to be easy became the toughest thing for us. A kid's persistent no can be so annoying for us, but we have a lesson to learn from them when it comes to this.

My 16-month-old daughter makes it clear if she's not interested in something. Without hesitation, she'll say no and walk away or turn her head. I respect her 'no' unless there's an immediate danger or an unsafe situation.

It's time to tap into that toddler in us who loved saying no and combine it with the tact of an adult. I'm listing some techniques that will help you embrace 'no' with confidence, ease, and positivity.

1. The Empathetic Decline

When you find yourself needing to say no in situations where you know the other person might feel disappointed, begin with empathy.

Show them that you heard their request, acknowledge it, and repeat it so that they know you understood. Then, decline gently and immediately offer a reason why you won't be able to fulfil their request.

Try this: "I completely understand that it is a special day for you, and we would have loved to be there, but unfortunately, we can't make it. We made plans a month ago that we can't change."

2.   The Grateful No

This is when you begin by expressing your gratitude and showing appreciation for the request the other person put forth. After you thank them, clearly but politely decline, giving your reasons.

Show gratitude once again to show that you truly value their invitation or request, but it's just not the right time for you.

People respond well to gratitude, and when you give a genuine reason, they will not feel too upset about you declining their invitation or request.

Try this: "Thank you so much for thinking of me and inviting me to join the committee. I'm honoured by the invitation, and I appreciate the opportunity. However, due to my current commitments, I won't be able to take on any additional responsibilities at this time. I'm really grateful for your understanding."

3.   The Delayed Response

Once you get a request from someone and you aren't sure whether you want to accept the invitation or request, ask them for some time to consider the request.

This will give you ample time to think things through, look at your priorities and schedule, and respond with a well-thought-out answer. You can use your scripts here if you do decide to say no.

The 'Let-me-check-my-schedule' technique works well as it buys you time to check your availability and make an informed decision. You don't have to explicitly say no initially.

Try this: "I'd like to help, but I need to check my schedule first. I'll get back to you soon."

4.   The "I" Statements

We have seen many examples of how to use "I" statements and why they work. Remember, when you use these statements, explain your side of the story and show them your perspective and why you need to decline.

Focus the conversation on your feelings.

Try this: "I'm sorry, but I cannot come out for dinner right now. I'm really tired and will be sleeping early tonight. I can catch up sometime later this week. You guys have fun!"

5.   The Alternative Suggestion

Use this every single time, whenever possible, if you say no using any of the methods we discussed till now.

After you say no, offer them an alternative. This method ensures that even when you decline, the other person gets some sort of help or assistance with their request.

Try this: "I'm sorry I won't be able to lend you that because of (state your reason), but I'm more than happy to suggest where you can buy them from or give you any other pair you like."

6.   The Clear and Direct No

Sometimes, you have to say a straightforward no. You know that in certain situations, no amount of genuine reasoning, explanations, or elaboration would work. In such cases, just stick to simple, firm, polite no.

You must have heard this a million times – No is a complete statement. So, use it as a full statement without feeling bad if you are confident in your no.

If they refuse to understand or try to guilt you without making any effort on their end, it's a 'they' problem, not a 'you' problem. Don't worry too much about it.

Try this: "No, I won't do that."

7.   The "Yes, But..." Technique

A lot of improvisational theatre artists use the 'yes and' technique, where they accept and build upon what another person has said or suggested. Professionally, it's a great way to show their creativity because it helps to keep the flow of ideas going rather than shutting them down.

It is a great way to encourage a more open and inclusive dialogue, which is why a slight modification to it can work well for boundary setting too.

To use the 'yes, but' technique, first listen to the presented request or argument and say 'yes' to show that you understand the other's perspective. Then, follow that with 'but' and put it in your perspective. This allows the other person to get both perspectives, and it works when they don't have an idea of what you're thinking or your perspective.

Try this: "Yes, I understand that this trip is important to you, but I have some work commitments that I cannot move around this time. But do share the pics because would love to see them."

The Sandwich Method

We have discussed 7 ways to say no. You can combine either of these techniques into a 'sandwich method'. It's a very common technique, especially used by teachers or managers while giving feedback. You can easily extend this for boundary setting too.

One of my favourite school teachers consistently employed this method while providing feedback. Looking back, I realize this is why we held her in high regard— she corrected us without diminishing our confidence. In contrast, other teachers would often scold us for mistakes without offering constructive feedback.

This is how it's done.

Let's take an example of someone inviting you to a celebratory party that you won't be able to attend.

Start the conversation with something positive, like congratulating them for the occasion they invited you to.

Following it with your 'no' in any of the above mentioned ways.

And immediately follow it with another positive thing like offering an alternative, commenting that you wish you were there, or thanking them once again for thinking of you.

In the sandwich technique, you are cushioning one 'no' with two positive things. This reduces the chances of others feeling bad about the 'no'.

Select the method based on the situation and your relationship dynamics with the person making the request. Throughout the process, maintain empathy and respect.

Even if the other person isn't being understanding or respectful, stand your ground firmly and politely. Over time, people will recognize your commitment to boundaries, and it will become a normal part of your interactions.

The first few times may be rough on everyone, and it's expected. That's the 'teething pain' phase of boundary setting. But when you are consistent enough, it becomes normal for everyone involved in the process, and you won't have to repeat your boundaries time and again.

And when that happens, all the guilt, awkwardness, shame, and fear will go out of the window.

ACTIVITY 12: Do a Boundary Check-In

When you started this book, did you define any boundaries for yourself? If yes, then now might be a good time for a check-in.

- Reflect on whether any of the boundaries that you had set worked well or not. Were your boundaries accepted or violated and challenged?

- If you're having trouble remembering, go back to your emotions and feelings again. Check if you got angry, exhausted, burnt out, resentful, stressed, or fearful in any situation. Analyse if it was due to boundary violation, others' negative reactions to the boundaries, or your inability to set or communicate boundaries well.

- Once you identify such scenarios, try to pinpoint what exactly went wrong. Do you identify any specific challenges? Did you refrain from setting boundaries because you were afraid of conflict? Because you weren't confident to communicate assertively, or the situation spiralled because you got aggressive? Or, you forgot what to say, let others violate the boundaries, didn't maintain the boundary or hold any consequence?

This step will give you a clear idea of what you need to work on going ahead.

You can download boundary check-in reflection questions from my website if you need a little assistance to do this activity. You can find it here - https://alekhyakoruti.com/say-yes-to-you-landing-page#freedownloads.

Clearly outline the challenges you are facing. Then, assess which of the solutions we've discussed can be applied to address each specific challenge. If you forgot what to say or fumbled a lot because of which you couldn't get your point across clearly, then you need to practice the boundary scripts more.

If you weren't assertive enough, that's your cue to practice assertive communication. If you had trouble handling some emotions, identify which emotion it was and try the associated strategies to manage that.

Now you are aware of what exactly needs your attention. So, just tackle it head-on and practice a lot. Just like any other area, setting effective boundaries needs lots and lots of practice.

At the same time, it is important that you make realistic action plans. You cannot try to tackle all challenges at once. Break down a big boundary into small steps. Increasing boundary setting practices gradually will be easier for you and others, and result in higher success too.

Don't make the mistake of setting all the firm or red boundaries for everyone at the same time. You will end up feeling very isolated and misunderstood. It's only fair that you give the other person some time to get used to the boundary. The only thing in your control is to maintain your boundaries, so just focus on that.

At this point, I would like to repeat again that you need to have consequences for boundary violation. Don't feel awkward about that. When you let others violate the boundary and don't do anything about it; it will repeat. That's a given.

For instance, if your team member is repeatedly violating boundaries related to work responsibilities, you can consider reassigning their projects to those demonstrating greater respect for established boundaries.

In a scenario where, financial boundaries are at stake, you can consider limiting financial support and help them in any other way until they demonstrate responsible financial behaviour.

Or, when someone blatantly disregards your boundaries of not sharing private information with others, you can stop sharing such details with them until they make changes.

Seeking Support

Here's one thing that most people get wrong about boundary setting – that you have to do it alone. That's so far from the truth. There will be someone, even if it's the one person you didn't expect, to support you through this. Don't hesitate to seek support and build a security blanket of these people who can help you through this journey. It will do wonders for your boundary setting journey.

There are two ways you can seek support.

Boundary Buddies

You are aware of them. I've mentioned them throughout the book. You need to have at least one boundary buddy; having a few is awesome. These are individuals who will help you establish and maintain your boundaries, act as a sounding board, team up to practice boundary scripts, and be someone to lean on when you are feeling negative emotions.

Boundary buddies can be your friends, family, mentors, or anyone that you trust has your best interest in their hearts. These individuals will also give you accountability, different perspectives, and guidance if and when you need it.

Samir, a software engineer, found himself overwhelmed with work demands and struggling to set boundaries with his demanding manager. The constant pressure was taking a toll on his mental health.

Recognizing the need for change, he decided to confide in his friend, Madhu, whom he considered a trusted boundary buddy.

Madhu, having experienced similar challenges in the past, empathized with Samir's situation. She not only listened attentively but also shared her own strategies for setting boundaries at work. Encouraged by Madhu's insights, Raj decided to implement a few boundary-setting techniques discussed during their conversation.

Over the next few weeks, Samir gradually communicated his limits to his manager, set realistic expectations, and learned to say no when necessary. Having Madhu as his boundary buddy provided the support and accountability he needed. The positive changes in Raj's work-life balance were noticeable, and he felt more empowered and in control.

This story highlights the impact of having a boundary buddy who understands your struggles and provides guidance and encouragement, ultimately contributing to a healthier and more balanced life.

Professional Help

Prachi lit up any room she went to. People remembered her for how generous she was, how she honoured every single commitment she made, and how she went out of the way to help anyone who reached out to her. But nobody saw how much she was struggling. Not even her closest friends.

She had panic attacks, and now the frequency was increasing. It was becoming difficult to excuse herself every time she could feel a panic attack coming on. She was running on empty and was finding it tougher and tougher to show up for others. But she didn't know how to set boundaries. Or didn't want to for some of the many reasons we discussed until now.

She managed to hide it until she broke down right in the middle of a dinner party when someone put forth another request. Her friends immediately knew something was wrong when they saw mascara running down freely on her usually smiling face. She couldn't even get the words out for anyone to understand what was wrong. Luckily, her friends held space for her and let her cry it out. Later that night, she finally told one friend why she broke down.

The next day, she made her very first appointment with a therapist. The only thing that put Prachi through that experience was her lack of setting boundaries. She didn't even realise that she got depressed and exhausted by the constant giving. She had a wonderful set of friends who came together to support her. But they never knew how much she was struggling to maintain that persona everyone had of her – of someone who always showed up, was always there for everyone, and always went out of the way to help others.

No matter how good your support system is, there may be situations when boundary-related challenges and issues can get too complicated for them to handle. Or some situation may arise that can be too emotionally challenging for them to handle and support you at the same time.

If you are getting too stressed and are chronically anxious, boundary setting and violations can leave you in a state of heightened alertness, which can take a toll on you mentally. When it gets too much to handle, you may feel extreme physical symptoms that can leave you insomniac, with severe digestive distress or chronic migraines. And if your sense of powerlessness or identity loss reaches an extreme, it may lead to clinical depression too.

If you have difficulty setting boundaries due to some past trauma or unresolved issues or have been through a pattern of boundary violations that threaten your well-being or even physical safety, then there is very little that your loved ones can do to help you in a positive way except offer support.

The only way forward in such cases is to seek professional help. Don't look at it as a sign of weakness – remember that it is a sign of immense strength. Therapists and counsellors are qualified people who are trained to help individuals in these situations and they can help you manage your boundary setting and associated challenges in a constructive manner.

ACTIVITY 13 – Form Your Support System

Now that you know the importance of having a support system, let's make one for you.

- Identify people who can be your boundary buddies or those who can support you and reach out to them.

- Help them understand how they can assist you. This ensures they're prepared for any situation, preventing them from being surprised. If you don't communicate your needs, they might provide the wrong support or be unsure of what to do, potentially leaving them feeling helpless despite their genuine desire to help, which could worsen the situation for you.

- Also, keep a list of trained therapists near you just so that you have it ready.

- If you don't want to do this, ask someone from your support system to find a trained professional. It's always better to have it and not need it rather than needing it and not having it!

Managing emotions isn't always easy and can take time, but having the right support system can make all the difference.

So, make sure you surround yourself with trusted people.

Prachi is doing great now. By confiding in her friends what she was going through and using the tools her therapist gave, she finally learnt to balance self-care and showing up for others. She still goes out of her way to help others and be there when someone needs her, but she also knows where to draw the line and focus on herself when it gets too much for her.

Up until now, it was all about you. But we know that in the world of boundary setting, it takes two to tango. The next chapter is all about others and how you can play a supporting role.

*** *** ***

In a Nutshell

> There are 6 emotions commonly associated with boundary setting. Once you identify which one you feel, you can work on learning how to manage that.
> There are different ways to say 'no', all of which can be used in the sandwich technique.
> Don't hesitate to seek support, either from loved ones or professional therapists, if you find boundary-setting to be overwhelming.

ALEKHYA KORUTI

Identifying and Respecting Others' Boundaries

"You teach people how to treat you by what you allow, what you stop, and what you reinforce."

SAY YES TO YOU

- Tony Gaskins

9

Setting boundaries is a two-way street. I'm sure you know this by now.

We have discussed you being the boundary setter, but every day, you'll also find yourself on the other side of the line. The side where you have to recognise, acknowledge and respect others' boundaries. It is important that you don't lose sight of the fact that others have boundaries that you may not like.

We have also seen how to set boundaries in different areas of life. You now know how to ace setting personal boundaries or those with family, friends, work, and relationships. You must have already implemented some of the discussed tools and strategies or helping others do the same.

So, it wouldn't be a stretch for you to think that as someone championing boundary setting, you can honour others' boundaries easily. In most cases, you definitely will. But there is a chance, even if it's a small one, that you may unintentionally violate others' boundaries.

This chapter will talk about what you need to know or do when you have to find yourself in that sticky spot.

Let's start with understanding the very first step.

Identifying Others' Boundaries

It probably took you a while to get comfortable communicating your boundaries to someone. Or you could still be working on it. What if someone isn't on the same playing field and is uncomfortable or unable to explicitly communicate their boundaries? You know that even if they don't communicate, they will surely have some boundaries. So, how do you identify them?

I remember a situation with my former roommates that involved a minor disagreement. One of them, let's call her Y, had a friend visiting the city whom she invited to stay the night. Y was close to all of us, so she assumed none of us would mind, especially because it was for just one night. Most of us were okay with it, except for one roommate, let's call her Z.

Z had recently expressed her discomfort with frequent friend visits, especially overnight stays. While she didn't mind someone coming over for a few hours, she had requested no overnight stays, and we had agreed to respect that. Y had forgotten about that and unintentionally crossed this boundary, but as soon as she realized, she took responsibility. She acknowledged her mistake, apologised, and assured Z that it wouldn't happen again. Y even offered to stay in a hotel with her friend to avoid causing any discomfort.

Z appreciated the apology and told Y it was okay to bring her friend this one time. After this incident, such boundaries were never crossed again.

*** *** ***

I'm listing some tools and techniques to address the impact of crossing someone's boundary if you do find yourself in that situation. You don't have to use all of them; choose the ones that best fit the person and situation.

- Active listening: This is such a powerful, potent communication tool that many of us don't fully utilize. It's unfortunate that we often overlook its potential. The saying, "We often listen to reply, not to understand," highlights the essence of active listening. It means paying close attention when others speak, helping you grasp their comfort level with ongoing topics and the current situation. Techniques like paraphrasing, asking questions, and using non-verbal cues enhance your understanding of their perspective and help identify their boundaries.

- Consent and permission: These are a no-brainer. We must take consent or permission when it comes to sensitive topics or things that may be important to the other person. This applies to physical boundaries, emotional conversations, or when talking about shared experiences.

If you feel they are getting uncomfortable while talking about something, hit the brakes. Ask if they want to talk about something else and change the topic. Take permission if they are alright with you talking about a shared experience.

At the workplace, asking someone something that they legally cannot talk about because of confidentiality is crossing their boundaries.

- Look out for non-verbal cues: Some people may be uncomfortable talking about their boundaries, but they'll surely display non-verbal cues. Watch out for signs like appearing tense, stepping away to make a physical distance, avoiding eye contact, and withdrawing. All these are clear signs of non-verbal cues to show their boundaries. Look at their facial expressions and body language or posture.

- Ask open-ended questions: Open-ended questions encourage others to share freely and more openly about themselves because they are in control of what they are willing to share. In turn, it'll help you get a better understanding of their preferences and limits.

- Practice Empathy: This can help you put yourself in others' shoes, gaining a better understanding of their feelings, needs, and desires. Empathy is also crucial in gauging someone's boundaries and comfort levels, which in turn creates more meaningful connections.

- Set an example: If you feel someone is struggling to share their boundaries due to any negative or overwhelming emotion, start talking about your own boundaries if you can. This will help others feel comfortable enough to share their boundaries.

- Mutual agreement: In some cases, explicitly discussing about setting mutual boundaries can also be helpful. All the involved individuals can engage in a conversation and mutually agree on certain boundaries that everyone would adhere to.

- Never assume: You can be comfortable with something, but don't assume others feel the same way. Never assume that you know what's best for someone, even if you have the best intentions at heart. If you do have something in mind that could be construed as an assumption, it's better to tactfully put it out in the open and let the person share how they feel about it.

- Respect privacy: Don't share personal information, stories, or experiences of others without their permission. If someone confides in you and believes that you will not share it with anyone, don't think it's okay to share that with someone who's not a mutual friend. It is a huge boundary violation.

- Be flexible: Understand that others' boundaries are flexible and can change over time. If someone was flexible with a particular boundary sometime back but is more rigid about it now, respect that and don't question it. Adapt to these changes and keep an open line of communication to understand how you can better support their boundaries.

- Educate yourself: Some boundaries are a part of the cultural and social norms that one grows up in. If you have family or friends belonging to a different culture, educate yourself so that you can better understand their innate cultural boundaries. Being aware of these boundaries can help you navigate relationships with more sensitivity.

For instance, some cultures have specific guidelines on clothing or accessories that they should wear. Questioning that is a boundary violation. If you're unaware, ask them to share about it, and they'll happily do it. Or, you could educate yourself about the time boundaries that can differ between cultures. Some cultures prioritize punctuality, while others may have a more relaxed attitude toward time. If you are aware beforehand, you won't risk violating someone's time boundary.

Above all, prioritize self-care. Lean on your self-care toolkit to maintain your emotional and mental well-being. When you focus on your well-being, you will be better equipped to respect the boundaries of others.

What to Do When You Violate Someone's Boundaries

It was Kirti's birthday, and her sister Kiran decided to throw a surprise party. Kiran invited Kirti's closest friends to her favourite restaurant. However, what Kiran overlooked was that Kirti, being an introvert, preferred more low-key celebrations.

As the surprise party unfolded, Kiran could see Kirti getting overwhelmed and not enjoying the grand celebration at all. It dawned on her that she had crossed her sister's boundary by planning a public event when Kirti would have preferred a quiet, private evening.

After the party, Kiran had an open conversation with Kirti. She apologized for not respecting her sister's preferences and asked what type of celebration she would enjoy in the future. Kirti appreciated Kiran's understanding and thanked her for her sincerity. They mutually agreed to plan a more suitable celebration for Kirti's next birthday.

This incident serves as an example of a boundary violation that didn't result in a serious fallout between the sisters. While Kirti was initially upset and angry, she understood that Kiran's intentions were good. The post-violation repair didn't take too long.

However, such understanding and quick resolution may not always be the case in every boundary violation.

The extent of harm caused by a boundary violation can vary depending on different factors. Intentional boundary violations are typically very damaging, but even accidental or unintentional violations can still hurt someone.

We'll look at techniques to diffuse a tense situation caused by boundary violation and some conflict resolution techniques that can help in recovering and rebuilding trust and fostering healthy relationships.

You may hope to never use these actionable tools, but it doesn't hurt to know them in case you have to use them when needed.

1. Immediately acknowledge the violation. Even if it was unintentional, don't deny or ignore it. Recognize that you messed up and let the other person know the same.

2. Offer sincere apologies. Do not apologise half-heartedly or for the sake of it just because you feel you did it unintentionally. If you think apologising in the current moment won't be taken well because of high emotions, apologize quickly and come back when they are calmer.

3. Don't get defensive or justify your actions. Practice active listening and hold space for them to express themselves freely about how they are feeling. Ask what you can do to make them feel better.

4. Be open to understanding their perspective. You may find someone's boundary unreasonable or small and feel that their reaction to you violating the boundary was much

bigger than necessary. But for them, it would be a huge deal. If you try to think from their perspective, you may get a better understanding of the impact of your actions and possibly their huge reaction.

5. Respect their decision, even if it goes against what you had hoped for. Sometimes, people may not respond well to your apology and react by doing something that you may not like. For instance, choosing to be alone for a few days or limiting conversation with you.

   If you have done everything you could do to repair the situation and they still need some distance, respect that. Give them the space to process their emotions and get back to you. Don't hold it against them that since you apologized, they should forgive and move on quickly.

6. Give it time. Sometimes, the boundary violation could be too huge for someone where they feel their trust was broken or they feel incredibly hurt. Rebuilding trust after such a scenario may take time. So, try to be patient. If possible, you can demonstrate through actions that you are willing to do whatever it takes from your end to repair the relationship and do it. But again, don't push the other person too much.

7. Seek support: If you are struggling to understand someone's boundaries, don't hesitate to seek help and support from a trusted person.

Once again, it's important to prioritize self-care to process your own emotions. Being someone who unintentionally violates boundaries can be rough on you, especially when you champion and advocate for boundary setting. But don't be too hard on yourself. Accept that everyone makes mistakes and that it is inevitable. How you respond after a boundary violation will be more important than beating yourself up.

Do take some time to reflect on why you possibly crossed someone's boundaries. Was it because you were unaware of them, or were you aware, but in the heat of the moment, your actions were different than normal? Or was there any other reason?

Reflecting will give you a deeper understanding of your own behaviours and help you avoid and prevent further boundary violations. It'll help if you consider this as a learning moment. Mistakes happen, but if you don't learn from them, you'll repeat them. Use this incident as an opportunity to grow and get a deeper understanding of others' boundaries and respect them.

Once the situation has calmed down, be open to discussing boundaries in a respectful way. You can clarify their limits, reinforce your limits, and even discuss how to avoid future violations. Establish very clear boundaries for the future for both of you. Honest communication is the only way forward.

Conflict Resolution

Boundary violations can often result in conflicts. While we previously discussed a technique specifically for familial conflicts, here are some broad strategies that apply to conflicts with anyone.

You can use these techniques to address conflicts that arise as a result of you violating someone else's boundary or someone violating yours.

- Stay calm: It's important that you keep your emotions in check. Responding with anger or frustration will only escalate the conflict instead of resolving it. Try to remain calm and composed during the conflict.

- Assertive communication: When a boundary is crossed, use assertive communication to express your discomfort or objection. Be direct and clear about your boundaries and how they were violated or why you violated someone's boundaries and how you intend to correct it.

- Stay focused: In the heat of the moment, it is possible to deviate from the topic. Ensure you keep the discussion focused on boundary violation. Avoid any mention of a past conflict or unrelated issues.

- Take a break: If the fight gets too intense, it's wise to take a break to collect your thoughts and manage emotions. Taking a break can prevent you from saying things that you may regret later.

- Avoid blame: It's easy to point fingers in the middle of an argument, but assigning blame will not help anyone. Try to keep the conversation on how you can resolve the boundary violation issue instead of analysing who was at fault.

- Find common ground: Identify what solutions to the conflict are mutually acceptable for both parties involved. You can look into shared goals and interests to identify the common ground and reach a solution.

- Use 'STOP' phrases: If someone is crossing a boundary again during a fight, firmly say 'stop,' 'that's not acceptable,' or 'I can't allow that.' This will prevent further boundary violations and escalate the conflict.

- Redefine the boundary: If necessary, clarify or redefine the boundaries in the midst of the conflict so that it offers clarity as to why the violation upset you. Reminding this could de-escalate the conflict and prevent it from deviating from the topic.

- State the impact: Try to explain how the boundary violation made you feel. Conveying the impact can help the other person understand the consequences of their actions or how it affects you, whether you are the one whose boundaries were violated or if you unintentionally violated their boundaries.

- Seek agreement: Don't carry the conflict for too long. Express your intention to reach an agreement on how to respect each other's boundaries going ahead.

- Fight right: Respect their boundaries even amid heightened emotions. A fight isn't an invitation to cross their boundaries or make personal attacks.

Boundary setting has a learning curve for everyone involved. No matter how much of a pro you are at setting boundaries and understanding the intricacies of everything involved in it, there are chances that you will, at some point, violate someone's boundary unintentionally.

If that happens, give yourself grace, apply the strategies, and move forward with understanding.

Well, guess what? We are on the final stretch now. The last chapter explores the enjoyable side of setting boundaries. Believe it or not, there's a fun aspect to the world of boundaries!

*** *** ***

In a Nutshell

> Learning to identify others' boundaries and respecting them is as important as setting boundaries for yourself.
> Apply different tools and techniques to recognize others' boundaries.
> There are ways to recover and rebuild trust if you do violate someone's boundaries unintentionally.
> Don't be afraid of conflicts. Instead, try to learn how to resolve them positively.

The Way Ahead With Boundaries

"Your time and energy are precious. Set boundaries and guard them with your life."

—   Brian Tracy

10

You've done it!

You took the first step to learn how to set boundaries and probably implemented some tools and strategies that you think would work for you.

It's time to pat yourself on the back. Wherever you are, do it right now. Don't worry about it looking silly. Just do it, please.

Wonderful!

Now, don't think your job here is done. Setting boundaries is not a single, isolated activity where you do it once and never look at it again. Throughout the book, we have seen that boundaries are flexible and that they will keep changing. So, keep adapting your boundaries as your life evolves.

Now, your most important task lies ahead. Two actually.

First, you already know because it has come in every single chapter, but I have to reinforce it once again before we part – Maintain your boundaries. We'll see how to do that in a bit.

For now, let's jump right into the second task because it's my favourite! And that is - celebrating the wins. No matter how small they may seem, you have to celebrate them. Well, come to think of it, when it comes to boundary setting, there are no 'small' wins. Every win is massive. Every step you've taken is a step toward a healthier, more balanced life.

So, celebrate like no one's watching.

Recognize your Progress

It is very easy to get consumed by the process of boundary setting and everything associated with it that you may not even realise how far you've actually come. At the beginning of this book, you may have been a complete novice, but now, even if you haven't completely mastered it, I'm pretty sure you must have made some progress.

The tools and techniques I've shared are exactly the ones that I applied to master boundary setting. I've helped many people through this and they have seen some awesome changes. So, if you've tackled these exercises, you should be noticing some real progress.

Take a moment to acknowledge that. This may not have been an easy journey for you, but even taking one step is a huge deal, and that deserves a celebration.

So, let's do that first.

ACTIVITY 14: Celebrate

Dance, order your favourite food, or pamper yourself in whatever way you like. Celebrate the way you want, but make sure to celebrate each and every milestone.

Recognizing even the smallest milestone will boost your self-esteem and motivate you to continue your boundary setting journey with success. Said 'no' once to an extra work assignment? That's a win. Had a tough conversation with someone about a boundary you wish to set? That's a win.

Do not underestimate the power of celebrating small wins in boundary setting. Here are some ideas to get you started.

- Self-reflection ritual: This could be a weekly or monthly thing where you reflect upon the boundary setting success you had that week/month. Consider the tiniest of wins.

- Symbolic celebration: You can associate something tangible with a boundary setting win. It could be a simple tick mark on paper, buying something you like, having some chocolate or ice cream, or doing some self-indulgence activity.

- Reward system: If you like competition, you can create a reward system for yourself. You can gamify the whole process and choose boundary milestones for yourself. Each time you check off a milestone, treat or reward yourself with something special.

- Share it: You can even share your wins with your boundary buddy or support system. Celebrating on your own is great, but it gets even more special when a loved one celebrates your achievements

- Boundary Playlist: Music is a huge mood booster and can act as a great motivator. Create a playlist of songs that make you feel empowered and confident. Listen to them before setting boundaries or to celebrate your progress by dancing it out!

Beyond the celebrations, you have to take one final step.

The nature of boundary setting is that it's a continuous process; it would benefit if you have a 'boundary maintenance' plan in place. Just to make it easy.

Boundary Maintenance

You definitely understand by now that you absolutely need to maintain your boundaries. If you don't stick to them, this could be a very long, disappointing process.

This is why you need the 'Boundary Maintenance Plan'.

It will ensure you stay accountable and allow you to track progress. A structured plan can help you manage your time and tasks in a manner that supports your well-being.

There are some key components of this plan. This is everything we have already seen, but a quick recap will be ideal here.

Clear boundaries: While it might seem repetitive, emphasizing the importance of setting and communicating clear boundaries is crucial. A solid foundation makes it easier to maintain boundaries and handle conflicts and misunderstandings like a pro.

Self-care routine: You need to manage your emotional well-being at every stage of boundary setting. A solid self-care routine will make the process a little smoother to navigate. Include mood-boosting and calming activities like exercising, mindfulness, journaling, hobbies, etc., to prioritise yourself. Remember, it's not wrong to prioritise yourself. You deserve to be happy.

Support systems: Boundary setting can be very intimidating in the beginning, and even if it's easy, it's better to have someone in your corner. Lean on friends, family, or professional help like a therapist if needed, but do build a strong support system around you. It makes a world of difference. They can help you maintain boundaries and offer guidance and accountability while providing a safe space.

Additionally, you may need to actively develop certain skills, especially if they're not your strong suit. Though they might seem unrelated to boundary setting, believe me, honing these skills will be truly beneficial.

1. Goal Setting: If you look at it, setting a boundary for your well-being needs to be treated as a goal. So, why not use tools like SMART goals for it? When you take a step in setting a boundary, ensure it is specific, measurable, achievable, relevant, and time-bound. This approach provides clarity and ensures your efforts are focused and effective.

2. Time Management: This is a crucial part of boundary setting. Time management will help you stick to your boundaries, prevent burnout, and reduce stress. For instance, when you want to set a hard boundary at work that you need to leave by a certain time every day, you need to ensure that you have strong time management skills to finish off the work within that time frame. This will allow you to actively allocate time for self-care instead of it becoming an afterthought.

3. Communication Skills: There are no points for guessing why this skill is important. Without effective communication skills, you will not be able to convey your boundaries, express your needs, desires, and emotions, be assertive, or respond to others' concerns in a firm, assertive, yet respectful manner. Boundary setting is all about promoting healthy relationships, and good communication skills support that.

4. Resilience and Adaptability: You need to be resilient when it comes to setting and maintaining boundaries. There are no two ways about it. If you don't have this trait, it's time to build it. There will be setbacks and situations that you need to bounce back from, and resiliency will help you do that quicker. Adaptability will ensure that you adjust your boundaries as and when circumstances require it. Both these traits or qualities can help you balance your priorities with other's needs, even in difficult situations.

5. Practice 'Review & Reflect': Reflection involves regular self-assessment and learning from your experiences. This quality helps you gain a deeper understanding of yourself and identify what works for you and what doesn't. This will help you make changes or refine your strategies and tools for successful boundary setting.

Now that you're in the loop on all the elements of a boundary maintenance plan let's dive in and create it.

ACTIVITY 15: Make a Boundary Maintenance Plan

Here's a template of a boundary maintenance plan to get you started. Feel free to make changes as you like.

Your Path to Healthy Boundaries and Well-Being

I. Clear Boundaries - List your clear boundaries, both personal and professional.

Boundary Type:
o Description:
o Importance:

Boundary Type:
o Description:
o Importance:

Boundary Type:
o Description:
o Importance:

II. Self-Care Routines - Specify self-care routines you'll integrate into your life.

Self-Care Activity:

o Frequency:

o Preferred Time:
o Importance:

Self-Care Activity:

o Frequency:
o Preferred Time:
o Importance:

Self-Care Activity:

o Frequency:
o Preferred Time:
o Importance:

III. Support Networks - Identify individuals or groups that constitute your support network

Support Person/Group:
o Role:
o Contact Information:

Support Person/Group:
o Role:
o Contact Information:

Support Person/Group:
o Role:
o Contact Information:

IV. Goal Setting - Set SMART goals for maintaining your boundaries.

o Specific Goal:
o Measurable Outcome:
o Achievability:
o Relevance to Boundaries:
o Time Frame:

o Specific Goal:

o Measurable Outcome:
o Achievability:
o Relevance to Boundaries:
o Time Frame:

o Specific Goal:
o Measurable Outcome:
o Achievability:
o Relevance to Boundaries:
o Time Frame:

V. Review and Updates - Outline how often you'll review and update your Boundary Maintenance Plan.

o Review Frequency:
o Date of Next Review:

Use this template as a tool for structuring your ongoing boundary-setting efforts. Modify or make changes as you wish based on the boundaries you set. It will help you maintain clarity about your boundaries, prioritize self-care, engage your support network, and work towards specific goals that enhance your overall well-being.

Remember to revisit and update your plan regularly to adapt to changing circumstances and continue your journey towards healthy boundaries and a fulfilling life.

You are almost at the end of the finish line. But before I take your leave, I would like to remind you to do the activities mentioned in the book without fail, along with practicing boundary scripts and role-playing with your boundary buddies. They hold the key to successful boundary setting.

So, let's take a quick look at them once again.

Recap of All Activities

None of the activities shared in the book are a one-time activity. You must revisit them frequently and make changes as needed.

Whenever any boundary evolves, do the relevant activity, and don't forget to review it regularly.

Activity 1	The Garden Fence Exercise to Identify Your Boundaries
Activity 2	Assess Your Values and Priorities
Activity 3	Make Your Self-Care Toolkit
Activity 4	List Your Non-Negotiables
Activity 5	Write Boundary Scripts Based on Non-Negotiables
Activity 6 (Repeating activity)	Role-Play
Activity 7	Make Your Traffic Light System
Activity 8	The 24-Hour Rule
Activity 9	Expectation Setting Exercise
Activity 10	Social Commitment Audit
Activity 11	Make Assertive Refusal Boundary Scripts
Activity 12	Do a Boundary Check-In/ Boundary Review
Activity 13	Form Your Support System

Activity 14	Celebrate
Activity 15	Make/Revise your Boundary Maintenance Plan

And that brings us to the end of this journey.

Moving Forward

Congratulations once again on reaching this milestone!

Whether you are just starting boundary setting or honing the skill, your intention to understand and implement boundary-setting techniques is truly commendable. All the tools and strategies shared throughout the book are invaluable and versatile. They are interconnected, so use them the best way you think they can serve you.

Continue to apply them purposefully and strategically. They can really change your life and make it better and balanced.

Since boundaries are dynamic and ever-evolving, you will never truly be *done* with boundary setting, but it'll start coming as second nature to you. As you continue on this journey, do so with unwavering confidence and determination.

The path ahead is yours to shape.

Good luck!

*** *** ***

In a Nutshell

> Celebrate every win, no matter how small it is.
> Make a boundary maintenance plan to ensure you are able to sustain the boundaries you worked so hard on setting.

> Learn associated skills like time management and goal setting to enhance your success in setting boundaries.
> Don't view boundary setting as a chore. Have fun with it, and it'll improve your life.

Afterword

I truly hope this book has left a positive mark on your life, nudging you towards the realisation that boundaries are absolute game-changers. Even if you haven't taken the plunge into setting them just yet, I hope you're comfortable with the idea of boundary setting, free from guilt, hesitation, or fear.

Consider this book to be your trusty companion as you embark on this transformative journey. But if you feel that you need more help and support, I'm here for you! Sign up for my personalized 1:1 sessions or join the boundary-setting workshops that I regularly conduct.

For more details, visit www.alekhyakoruti.com or shoot me an email at connect@alekhyakoruti.com. Can't wait to connect and help you ace this essential skill!

About the Author

Alekhya has always followed her dreams and passions, which led her to make a career in writing after two short corporate stints post engineering. After a decade of freelancing for clients across the world, she pursued an MBA hoping to give the corporate world a try.

But life clearly had other plans. She welcomed her beautiful daughter and quickly realised that the corporate life was never meant for her. While thoroughly enjoying the new role as a mom, Alekhya found her true calling of empowering others, especially mothers with little to no support, and women who may feel lost or are having a tough time finding their purpose and passion.

Now, as a Certified Mindset, Parenting, and Life Coach, she's on a mission to spread the wisdom and skills she's gathered along the way. In a world that often feels lonelier despite being more connected than ever, she aims to make a difference and bring a bit more joy to people's lives.

When she is not working on her mission or playing with her toddler, she enjoys working out, daydreaming about where to travel next, and finding the answers to the hundred whys and hows that circle her mind.

www.ingramcontent.com/pod-product-compliance
Lightning Source LLC
Chambersburg PA
CBHW070928260726

48661CB00003B/881